MW01252723

# ĠHĀLIB

IN TRANSLATION

# ḠHĀLIB

## IN TRANSLATION

O. P. Kejariwal

UBSPD

UBS Publishers' Distributors Pvt. Ltd.

New Delhi • Bangalore • Chennai • Calcutta • Patna • Kanpur

UBS PUBLISHERS' DISTRIBUTORS PVT. LTD.

5 Ansari Road, New Delhi-110 002
Phones: 3273601, 3266646 • Cable: ALLBOOKS • Fax: 3276593, 3274261
E-mail: ubspd@ubspd.com• Website: www.gobookshopping.com

10 First Main Road, Gandhi Nagar, Bangalore-560 009
Phones: 2253903, 2263901, 2263902 • Cable: ALLBOOKS
Fax: 2263904 • E-mail: ubspd.bng@bgl.vsnl.net.in

60 Nelson Manickam Road, Aminjikari, Chennai-600 0029
Phones: 3746222, 3746287• Cable: UBSIPUBS • Fax: 2263904
E-mail: ubspd.che@eth.net

8/1-B Chowringhee Lane, Kolkata-700 016
Phones: 2441821, 2442910, 2449473 • Cable: UBSIPUBS
Fax: 2450027 • E-mail: ubspdcal@calvsnl.net.in

5 A Rajendra Nagar, Patna-800 016
Phones: 672856, 673973, 686170 • Cable: UBSPUB • Fax: 686169
E-mail: ubspdpat1@sancharnet.in

80 Noronha Road, Cantonment, Kanpur-208 004
Phones: 369124, 362665, 357488 • Fax: 315122
E-mail: ubsknp@sancharnet.in

Distributors for Western India:
M/s Preface Books
Unit No. 223 (2nd floor), Cama Industrial Estate,
Sun Mill Compound, Lower Parel (W), Mumbai-400 013
Phones: 022-4988054 • Telefax: 022-4988048 • E-mail: Preface@vsnl.com



First Published 2002



Cover & Book Design: Dushyant Parasher

Printed at: International Print-O-Pac Limited, Okhla Industrial Area, Phase-1, New Delhi

*To Debleena for her constant life giving companionship for over three decades now*

# INTRODUCTION

A little over a century and three decades have passed since Mirza Ghalib's death but his poetry continues to sparkle in the imagination and common conversation of the Urdu-speaking people. His *ghazals* are sung at musical soirees across the sub-continent, academics discuss his poetry in learned gatherings, films and TV serials based on his life evoke popular response. As new translations of his poetry into English and other Indian languages appear regularly, the bibliography on Ghalib's life and works keeps getting longer and yet people, the literate and the illiterate alike, do not seem to tire of quoting from and interpreting and re-interpreting his works and his poetry.

One reason for this ever-increasing popularity of Ghalib's poetry may lie in his modernity and his ability to blend different literary cultures into a harmonious whole. Reading Ghalib becomes an experience in exploring new horizons; each reader discovers something anew, and each fresh reading throws open a new layer of meaning. Another reason for this near-universal appeal of his works might be found in the fact that Ghalib lived and wrote at a time when the sun was setting on the Mughal Empire and the British were firmly establishing themselves on the Indian soil. His life coincided with one of the most tumultuous periods of Indian history. And this shows in his writings.

Mirza Asadullah Khan Ghalib was born in Agra on 27 December 1797. His ancestors, of Turkish stock, had come to India in the second half of the eighteenth century, seeking their fortune in the Mughal Court. Ghalib was very proud of his ancestral lineage and years later would write to a friend:

> I am a Turk by race, my genealogy goes back to Pashang and Afrasiab. My forefathers and the Seljuks are of the same stock, and during the days of their glory they were military leaders as well as commanders-in-chief. But the days of prosperity passed, the era of adversity and misfortune commenced, they forgot brigandage and pillage, and the tribe took agriculture as its profession. Samarkand in the land of Turan became the shelter of my ancestors.

Not much is known of Ghalib's childhood in Agra except that he lost his father, Abdullah Beg Khan, at the age of five and his uncle, Nasrullah Beg, two years later. Ghalib grew up in his maternal grandparents' house and the family's wealth and influence were sufficient to provide him an education available to the sons of aristocratic Muslim families. He was taught Persian, some Arabic, logic, philosophy and medicine but it was in linguistics and literature, particularly Persian, that his talents blossomed. According to his own account, Ghalib was writing Persian poetry by the age of eleven and started writing Urdu verse some years earlier. There is no authentic mention of a mentor but Ghalib himself often spoke of a mysterious Zoroastrian teacher of Iranian origin, Abdus Samad, who reportedly stayed with him for two years, first in Agra and then in Delhi, and taught him the intricacies of Persian poetics.

In 1810, at the age of 13, Ghalib was married to the 11-year-old Umrao Begam, daughter of Nawab Illahi Baksh Khan, and moved to Delhi shortly afterwards. It is in Delhi that the poetic genius of Ghalib came to be noticed by the literati. In the beginning he would write in the abstract style of symbolist Persian poets like Shaukat Bukhari, Aseer and Bedil. As a result, his early poetry was complicated, sometimes incomprehensible, and came under attack by the critics. The Urdu verse of this period suffered from excessive Persianisation and Ghalib himself was aware of this:

*Tarz-e-Bedil mein Rekhtaa likhna*
*Asadullah Khan! Qayaamat Hai!*

(Writing Urdu Poetry in the style of Bedil/
O Asadullah Khan is well nigh impossible)

He would later revise, on the advice of his friends, his Urdu *Deewan,* first compiled in 1821, and this won him great acclaim. Ghalib's poetic contribution in Persian is five times larger than in Urdu but his reputation as one of the greatest poets rests mostly on his slim Urdu *Deewan*.

Life in Delhi, in spite of the proximity to the Mughal Court and his creative energy bursting at the seams, was not an easy one for Ghalib. A series of misfortunes stalked the poet from 1826 onwards. His father-in-law died, creditors pressed him and disputes arose over his share in the hereditary pension originally granted by the British to his uncle. A series of petitions and a very arduous trip to Calcutta failed to restore his pension to the original amount and as one misfortune followed another, he was imprisoned briefly on a charge of running a gaming-house.

Notwithstanding these miseries on the personal front, Ghalib continued to write, mostly verse in Urdu. Around this time, he also took to Urdu as the medium of letter-writing, and in the process set new standards for Urdu prose. He was commissioned to write a history of the Mughal dynasty by Bahadur Shah Zafar and later became the Emperor's *ustad*. The King of Oudh granted him an annual stipend and the ruler of Rampur became his *shagird*. When the Sepoy Mutiny broke out in May 1857, Ghalib, living in the heart of Delhi, witnessed the rebellion and the British response from close quarters. He would record his experiences in his Persian diary *Dashtambu*. Financial difficulties, ill health and his efforts to gain acceptance from the new rulers took their toll and Ghalib died on 15 February, 1869.

Great poets have always had many interpreters. No interpretation, no translation can ever be final. This translation of 200 selected couplets from Ghalib's Urdu *Deewan* is similarly an attempt to understand and present one of the greatest poets of India anew. This includes my earlier attempt to translate 100 couplets of Ghalib, which was published as *Ghalib: A Hundred Moods* by the Publications Division, Government of India. Some of them have been retained, some altered and many translated afresh. If this translation succeeds in evoking fresh interest among the new generation of readers about this great poet, that would be reward enough for me.

Colleagues and friends have helped me in finalizing the selection of couplets, checking the translations, vetting and proofing, calligraphy, typing and in various other ways. There are some, however, whom if I do not acknowledge, I would be doing injustice not only to them but even to myself. These are Rehman Farooqi, Abrar Ahmad, Anwar, Ateeq Ahmed, Kajal Das, Dr. A.K. Gupta, Bujha Singh, Y.R. Kapoor, Dushyant Parashar, Mohan Gupta, Sanjay Garg and Anshu Gupta. My special thanks also to Vivek Ahuja for, had it not been for him, the book would not have seen the light of the day. And finally for my wife, Debleena, I can only say that I can never repay in words the many ways she has helped the book to grow and be completed.

May 2002 O.P. Kejariwal

یہ نہ تھی ہماری قسمت کہ وصالِ یار ہوتا
اگر اور جیتے رہتے یہی انتظار ہوتا

yé na thī hamārī qismat ki visālé-yār hotā
agar aur jīté rahté yahī intézār hotā

It's just not my fate
That this wait
Should end
And we unite.
For even if this life
Were longer
Then longer
Would be the wait.

*ये न थी हमारी क़िस्मत कि विसाले[1]-यार होता*
*अगर और जीते रहते यही इन्तज़ार होता*

---

*1. मिलन*

ترے وعدے پہ جیے ہم تو یہ جان جھوٹ جانا
کہ خوشی سے مر نہ جاتے اگر اعتبار ہوتا

téré vādé pé jiyé ham, tō yé jān jhūṭ jānā
ki ḳhushī sé mar na jāté agar aitbār hotā

Wouldn't I have died
Of joy
If the promise you made
Was fulfilled?
It's the promise you made
And did not fulfil
That makes me live
And stay alive.

*तेरे वादे पे जिए हम, तो ये जान झूठ जाना*
*कि ख़ुशी से मर न जाते अगर एतबार होता*

کوئی میرے دل سے پوچھے ترے تیرِ نیم کش کو
یہ خلش کہاں سے ہوتی جو جگر کے پار ہوتا

koī méré dil sé pūchhé téré tīré-nīmkash ko
yé ḳhalish kahāñ sé hotī jo jigar ké pār hotā

That half-drawn bow
That arrow about to go
Oh, ask my heart
The joy of the wait
For had it passed
Right through the heart
That would be the end
Of all that wait
And all that joy.

*कोई मेरे दिल से पूछे तेरे तीरे-नीमकश[1] को*
*ये ख़लिश[2] कहां से होती जो जिगर के पार होता*

---

*1. आधा खींचा हुआ तीर 2. चुभन*

یہ کہاں کی دوستی ہے کہ بنے ہیں دوست ناصح
کوئی چارہ ساز ہوتا کوئی غم گسار ہوتا

yé kahāñ ki dostī hai kī bané haiñ dost nāséh
koi chārāsāẓ hotā koī g̱hamgusār hotā

Who needs a friend
When all he gives
Is counsel and advice?
For what I need
From a friend indeed
Is cure for my pain
And healing for my ill.

*ये कहां की दोस्ती है कि बने हैं दोस्त नासेह*
*कोई चारासाज़[1] होता कोई ग़मगुसार[2] होता*

---

*1. चिकित्सक2. दुख का साथी*

رگِ سنگ سے ٹپکتا وہ لہو کہ پھر نہ تھمتا
جسے غم سمجھ رہے ہو یہ اگر شرار ہوتا

ragé-sang sé ṭapaktā vo lahū ki phir na thamtā
jisé g͟ham samajh rahé ho yé agar sharār hotā

Even the stone
Would not have thrown
A spark of fire
But would have thrown
A stream of blood
Without a cease
Were I to inscribe
My grief on it.

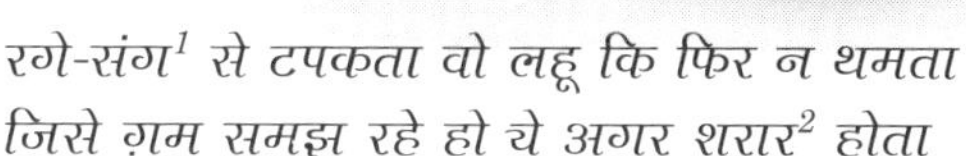
*रगे-संग[1] से टपकता वो लहू कि फिर न थमता*
*जिसे ग़म समझ रहे हो ये अगर शरार[2] होता*

---

*1. पत्थर की नस 2. चिंगारी*

غم اگرچہ جاں گسل ہے پہ کہاں بچیں کہ دل ہے
غمِ عشق گر نہ ہوتا، غمِ روزگار ہوتا

gẖam agarché jāngusil hai, pé kahāñ bachéñ ki dil hai
gẖamé-ishq gar na hotā, gẖamé-roz̤gār hotā

There is no escape
From the grief and pain
For one who has a heart.
For the heart would remain
Forever in pain
If not for love
Then
For the cares of the world.

*ग़म अगर्चे जांगुसिल[1] है, पे कहां बचें कि दिल है*
*ग़मे-इश्क़ गर न होता, ग़मे-रोज़गार[2] होता*

---

*1. कष्टदायक 2. संसार की चिंता*

کہوں کس سے میں کہ کیا ہے شبِ غم بری بلا ہے
مجھے کیا بُرا تھا مرنا اگر ایک بار ہوتا

kahūñ kisasé maiñ ki kyā hai shabé-ghạm burī balā hai
mujhé kyā burā thā marnā agar ék bār hotā

To whom can I explain
The grief and the pain
Which the night ushers in.
Indeed for me
What could better be
Than to court death?
But only if
The death could be
Only once
And once and for all.

*कहूं किससे मैं कि क्या है शबे-ग़म[1] बुरी बला है*
*मुझे क्या बुरा था मरना अगर एक बार होता*

---

*1. विरह की रात*

ہوئے مرکے ہم جو رُسوا ہوئے کیوں نہ غرقِ دریا
نہ کبھی جنازہ اُٹھتا نہ کہیں مزار ہوتا

hué marké ham jo rusvā hué kyūñ na g͟harqé-dariyā
na kabhī janāẓā uṭhtā na kahīñ maẓār hotā

Oh the shame in death
And the funeral bier
And the permanence of the shame
In the grave.
Only if I were
Drowned in the sea
There would be no funeral
No tomb
No grave.

हुए मरके हम जो रुसवा[1] हुए क्यूं न ग़र्के[2]-दरिया
न कभी जनाज़ा उठता न कहीं मज़ार होता

---

1. बदनाम 2. डूबना

اُسے کون دیکھ سکتا کہ یگانہ ہے وہ یکتا
جو دوئی کی بو بھی ہوتی تو کہیں دوچار ہوتا

usé kaun dékh saktā ki yagānā hai vo yaktā
jo duī kī bū bhī hotī tō kahīñ dochār hotā

He is the One
The only One
The Unique
And the Unseen.
For if there
Ever were
Yet another
Then certainly
Sometime somewhere
There would surely be
An encounter.

*उसे कौन देख सकता कि यगाना[1] है वो यक्ता[2]*
*जो दुई[3] की बू भी होती तो कहीं दोचार[4] होता*

---

*1. अद्वितीय 2. अकेला 3. द्वैत 4. आमने-सामने*

یہ مسائلِ تصوف، یہ ترا بیان غالب
تجھے ہم ولی سمجھتے، جو نہ بادہ خوار ہوتا

yé masāilé-tasavvuf̣, yé térā bayān 'Ġhālib'
tujhé ham valī samajhté, jo na bādā ḳhvār hotā

These matters abstruse
These thoughts divine
Your discussions on these
Would make thee O Ghalib
A saint sublime.
But all is lost in vain
For one weakness of thine
And that is
Your drowning in wine.

*ये मसाइले-तसव्वुफ़[1], ये तेरा बयान 'ग़ालिब'*
*तुझे हम वली समझते, जो न बाद:ख़्वार[2] होता*

---

*1. आध्यात्मिक विषयों की चर्चा 2. शराबी*

نہ تھا کچھ، تو خدا تھا، کچھ نہ ہوتا، تو خدا ہوتا
ڈبویا مجھ کو ہونے نے، نہ ہوتا میں، تو کیا ہوتا

na thā kuchh, tō Ḳhudā thā, kuchh na hotā, tō Ḳhudā hotā
ḍuboyā mujhko honé né, na hotā maiñ, tō kyā hotā

When there was nothing
There was God
If there would be nothing
There still would be God
Thus it is
The fact of being
Which is the cause
Of all my woes
What would have mattered
Indeed
Had I not been?

*न था कुछ, तो ख़ुदा था, कुछ न होता, तो ख़ुदा होता*
*डुबोया मुझको होने ने, न होता मैं, तो क्या होता*

ہوئی مدّت کہ غالبؔ مر گیا، پر یاد آتا ہے
وہ ہر اِک بات پر کہنا کہ یوں ہوتا تو کیا ہوتا

huī muddat ki 'Ġhālib' mar gayā, par yād ātā hai
vo har ik bāt par kahnā ki yūñ hotā tō kyā hotā

It's some time that Ghalib died
Yet is remembered
So widely
Especially his way
Of always asking
About everything
If this would have happened
Then what would have happened
And if that would have happened
*Then* what would have happened.

हुई मुद्दत कि 'ग़ालिब' मर गया, पर याद आता है
वो हर इक बात पर कहना कि यूं होता तो क्या होता

---

محبت تھی چمن سے لیکن اب یہ بے دماغی ہے
کہ موجِ بوئے گل سے ناک میں آتا ہے دم میرا

muhabbat thī chaman sé lékin ab yéh bédimāg͟hī hai
ki maujé-bū-é-gul sé nāk méiñ ātā hai dam mérā

There was a time
When I took delight
In the garden
With
Flowers and roses
But times have changed
And I am in a frame
Of mind that makes
Me turn away
In disgust
Even when roses are in bloom
And spread their fragrance
Everywhere.

*मुहब्बत थी चमन से लेकिन अब यह बेदिमाग़ी है*
*कि मौजे-बू-ए-गुल[1] से नाक में आता है दम मेरा*

---

*1. फूलों की सुगंध*

نقش، فریادی ہے کس کی شوخیِ تحریر کا
کاغذی ہے پیرہن ہر پیکرِ تصویر کا

naq̣sh, f̣ariyādī hai kiskī shoḳhié-taharīr kā
kāgḥẓī hai pairahan har paikaré-tasvīr kā

(Like in the Iran of old
A subject with a plaint
Written on raiment
Woven of paper
Appeared before
The Emperor)
So do I
Wear this raiment
Woven of paper
With every couplet
Being my plea
And my woe
That cries out for relief.

*नक़्श[1], फ़रियादी है किसकी शोख़िए-तहरीर[2] का*
*काग़ज़ी है पैरहन[3] हर पैकरे-तस्वीर[4] का*

---

*1. शारीरिक ढांचा 2. रचना की चंचलता 3. ईरान में यह रिवाज़ था कि फ़रियादी दरबार में काग़ज़ के कपड़े पहनकर आता था 4. चित्र का प्रकार*

خموشی میں نہاں خوں گشتہ لاکھوں آرزوئیں ہیں
چراغ مردہ ہوں میں بے زباں، گور غریباں کا

ḳhmoshī méiñ nihāñ, khūñ gashtā lākhoñ ārẓūéñ haiñ
charāgẖé-murdā hūñ, maiñ béẓubāñ, goré gẖarībāñ kā

In my silence
Lie my desires
By the myriads
Slain and dead.
And I remain
A blown-out lamp
Lone and alone
On a forlorn grave.

ख़मोशी में निहां[1], ख़ूं गश्ता[2] लाखों आरज़ूएं हैं
चराग़े-मुर्दा हूं, मैं बेज़ुबां, गोरे-ग़रीबां[3] का

1. छिपी हुई 2. जिसका ख़ून हो चुका हो 3. अनजान आदमी की कब्र

ہنوز اِک پرتوِ نقشِ خیالِ یار باقی ہے
دلِ افسردہ، گویا حجرہ ہے یوسف کے زنداں کا

hanoẓ ik partavé-naqshé k̤hyālé-yār bāqī hai
dilé-af̣surdā, goyā hujrā hai yūsuf̣ ké ẓindāñ kā

A heart full of dejection
And this dark prison cell !
But that ray of hope
Which brings back memories
Of you
Has turned this hole
Into the cell
Of Joseph.

*हनोज़*[1] *इक परतवे-नक़्शे-ख़्याले-यार*[2] *बाक़ी है*
*दिले-अफ़सुर्दा*[3], *गोया हुजरा*[4] *है यूसुफ़ के ज़िन्दां*[5] *का*

---

*1. अभी तक 2. कल्पना में प्रियतम की छवि का आभास 3. बुझा हुआ दिल*
*4. कोठरी 5. जेल*

حریفِ جوششِ دریا، نہیں خودداریِ ساحل
جہاں ساقی ہو تو، باطل ہے دعویٰ ہوشیاری کا

harīf̣é joshishé dariyā, nahīñ ḳhuddāri-é-sāhil
jahāñ sāq̣ī ho tū, bātil hai dāvā hoshiyārī kā

Can the river bank
Withstand
The onslaught of the tide?
And can one boast
Of sobriety
With the Saqi
Standing by?

*हरीफ़े-जोशिशे-दरिया[1], नहीं ख़ुद्दारि-ए-साहिल[2]*
*जहां साक़ी हो तू, बातिल[3] है दावा होशियारी का*

---

*1. दरिया के ज्वार का प्रतिद्वन्द्वी 2. तट का स्वाभिमान 3. बेमानी*

دل کو ہم صرفِ وفا سمجھے تھے، کیا معلوم تھا
یعنی، یہ پہلے ہی نذرِ امتحاں ہو جائے گا

dil ko ham sarf̣é-vaf̣ā samajhé thé, kyā mālūm thā
yāni, yé pahlé hī naẓré-imtihāñ ho jāégā

The heart, oh the heart
Once the symbol of loyalty
Alas has become
The first to be sacrificed
On the altar of love
In the test of loyalty.

दिल को हम सर्फ़े-वफ़ा[1] समझे थे, क्या मालूम था
यानी, ये पहले ही नज़्रे-इम्तिहां[2] हो जाएगा

---

1. वफ़ा मे न्योछावर 2. इम्तिहान की भेंट

گرچہ ہوں دیوانہ، پر کیوں دوست کا کھاؤں فریب
آستیں میں دشنہ پنہاں ہاتھ میں نشتر کھلا

garché hūñ dīvānā, par kyūñ dost kā khāūñ ḟaréb
āstīñ méiñ dashnā pinhāñ, hāth méiñ nashtar khulā

Granted I am mad
But should this mean
That I be deceived
By a friend
With a dagger up her sleeve
While on display
Is a lancet that heals?

*गर्चे हूं दीवाना, पर क्यूं दोस्त का खाऊं फ़रेब*
*आस्तीं में दश्ना[1] पिन्हां[2], हाथ में नश्तर[3] खुला*

---

*1. कटार 2. छिपी हुई 3. ख़ंजर*

ہے خیالِ حُسن میں حُسنِ عمل کا سا خیال
خلد کا اک در ہے میری گور کے اندر کھُلا

hai ḳhyālé husn méiñ husné-amal kā sā ḳhyāl
ḳhuld kā ik dar hai mérī gor ké andar khulā

Beauty is virtue
And beauty I pursued
And found a door
In my dark tomb
Open
On
To paradise.

*है ख़्याले-हुस्न में हुस्ने-अमल[1] का सा ख़्याल*
*ख़ुल्द[2] का इक दर है मेरी गोर[3] के अंदर खुला*

---

*1. नेक काम 2. स्वर्ग 3. समाधि*

در پہ رہنے کو کہا اور کہہ کے کیسا پھر گیا
جتنے عرصے میں مرا لپٹا ہوا بستر کھلا

dar pé rahné ko kahā aur kah ké kaisā phir gayā
jitné arsé méin mérā lipatā huā bistar khulā

And thus she changes
Her mind.
This moment
She tells me to stay
And before I unpack
She asks me
To go away.

दर पे रहने को कहा और कह के कैसा फिर गया
जितने अर्से में मेरा लिपटा हुआ बिस्तर खुला

تھی نوآموزِ فنا، ہمّتِ دشوار پسند
سخت مشکل ہے کہ، یہ کام بھی آساں نکلا

thī naūāmoẓé-f̣anā, himmaté-dushvār-pasand
saḳht mushkil hai ki, yéh kām bhī āsāñ nikalā

One would have thought
Surely nothing ought
To be more difficult
Than death itself
But now alas
Death itself
Has become so easy.

*थी नौआमोज़े-फ़ना[1], हिम्मते-दुश्वार-पसन्द[2]*
*सख़्त मुश्किल है कि, यह काम भी आसां निकला*

---

*1. मौत से अनजान 2. जिसको मुश्किलें पसन्द हो*

ذکر اُس پری وش کا، اور پھر بیاں اپنا
بن گیا رقیب آخر، تھا جو رازداں اپنا

ẓikr us parīvash kā, aur phir bayāñ apnā
ban gayā raqīb āḳhir, thā jo rāẓdāñ apnā

There was some talk
Of the lovely nymph
When for one
Did I butt in
And in a moment
Found my friend
With whom I shared
Secrets of my heart
Turn into a rival
And a deadly foe.

*ज़िक्र उस परीवश[1] का, और फिर बयां अपना*
*बन गया रक़ीब[2] आख़िर, था जो राज़दां[3] अपना*

---

*1. सुन्दरी 2. प्रेम में विरोधी 3. भेद जानने वाला*

منظر اک بلندی پر اور ہم بنا سکتے
عرش سے اِدھر ہوتا کاش کہ مکاں اپنا

manẓar ik bulandī par aur ham banā sakté
arsh sé idhar hotā kāsh ki makāñ apnā

No matter how far
The eyes can see
There's still the limit
Of the azure skies.
Were I to build a house
I would build a house
From where I could see
Beyond the stars
Beyond the skies.

*मंज़र[1] इक बुलन्दी पर और हम बना सकते*
*अर्श[2] से इधर होता काश कि मकां अपना*

---

*1. दृश्य 2. आकाश*

دردِ دل لکھوں کب تک، جاؤں اُن کو دکھلا دوں
انگلیاں فِگار اپنی، خامہ خونچکاں اپنا

dardé-dil likhūñ kab tak, jāūñ unko dikhlā dūñ
uñgaliyāñ figār apni, khāmā khūñ-chakāñ apnā

How long should I write
My tale of grief ?
Were it not better
That I should go
To her door
And do show
My heart that's sore
And my pen
Which only writes
As if with blood.

दर्दे-दिल लिखूं कब तक, जाऊं उनको दिखला दूं
उंगलियां फ़िगार[1] अपनी, ख़ामा ख़ूं-चकां[2] अपना

---

1. घायल 2. ख़ून से भरी क़लम

ہم کہاں کے دانا تھے! کس ہنر میں یکتا تھے
بے سبب ہوا غالبؔ دشمن آسماں اپنا

ham kahāñ ké dānā thé kis hunar méiñ yaktā thé
bésabab huā 'Ghālib' dushman āsmāñ apnā

I was neither so gifted
Nor so wise
In any of the arts
Then why, O why
Should the sky
Be so hostile
And make this life
O Ghalib
Full of misery?

*हम कहां के दाना[1] थे किस हुनर में यक्ता[2] थे*
*बेसबब हुआ 'ग़ालिब' दुश्मन आसमां अपना*

---

*1. बुद्धिमान 2. किस हुनर में माहिर*

رشک کہتا ہے کہ اس کا غیر سے اخلاص حیف
عقل کہتی ہے کہ وہ بے مہر کس کا آشنا

rashq kahatā hai ki uskā gẖair sé iḳhlās haif
aql kahatī hai ki vo béméhr kiskā āshnā

The envy
The jealousy
I harbour in my heart
Sighs when I see
Her with the other.
But silently then
The voice of reason
Says
How can it be
One as cold as she
Should love anyone
Could love anyone.

*रश्क़[1] कहता है कि उसका ग़ैर से इख़्लास[2] हैफ़[3]*
*अक़्ल कहती है कि वो बेमेह्र[4] किसका आशना[5]*

---

*1. ईर्ष्या 2. घनिष्ठता 3. हाय 4. निर्मोही 5. दोस्त*

میں، اور ایک آفت کا ٹکڑا وہ دلِ وحشی کہ، ہے
عافیت کا دشمن اور آوارگی کا آشنا

maiñ, aur ik āfat kā ṭukṛā vo dilé-vahshī ki, hai
āfiyat kā dushman aur āvāragī kā āshnā

This heart of mine
Wayward and wild
Enemy of peace
Condemning me
To endless wandering.

मैं, और इक आफ़त का टुकड़ा वो दिले-वहशी[1] कि, है
आफ़ियत[2] का दुश्मन और आवारगी का आशना

---

1. बेचैन दिल 2. शांति

بس کہ دشوار ہے ہر کام کا آساں ہونا
آدمی کو بھی میسّر نہیں انساں ہونا

bas ki dushvār hai har kām kā āsāñ honā
ādmī ko bhī mayassar nahīñ insāñ honā

How can
Everything
Become
So easy?
And so it is
Difficult indeed
For a man
To become
A human being.

*बस कि दुश्वार[1] है हर काम का आसां होना*
*आदमी को भी मयस्सर[2] नहीं इन्सां होना*

---

*1. मुश्किल 2. प्राप्त*

کی مرے قتل کے بعد اُس نے جفا سے توبہ
ہائے اُس زود پشیماں کا پشیماں ہونا

kī méré qatl ké bād usné jafā sé taubā
hāé us zūd pashémāñ kā pashémāñ honā

Yes she vowed
To shed
Her cruelty.
But by then
I had been
Slain!
And then to see
Her
In her repentance
She seemed a picture
Of repentance itself.

*की मेरे क़त्ल के बाद उसने जफ़ा[1] से तौबा*
*हाए उस ज़ूद पशेमां[2] का पशेमां होना*

---

*1. निर्दयता 2. तुरंत पछतावा होना*

حیف اس چار گرہ کپڑے کی قسمت غالبؔ
جس کی قسمت میں ہو عاشق کا گریباں ہونا

haiḟ us chār girah kapṛé kī qismat 'Ġhālib'
jiskī qismat méiñ ho āshiq kā garébāñ honā

Oh the pity
Of the shirt collar
Of the ardent lover
For it always remains torn.
For the beloved would tear
It in a frenzy
And the lover in pining
Despair and sorrow.

*हैफ़[1] उस चार गिरह कपड़े की क़िस्मत 'ग़ालिब'*
*जिसकी क़िस्मत में हो आशिक़ का गरेबां[2] होना*

---

*1. हाय 2. कुर्ते का ऊपरी हिस्सा*

در خورِ قہر و غضب جب کوئی ہم سا نہ ہوا
پھر غلط کیا ہے کہ ہم سا کوئی پیدا نہ ہوا

darḳhuré-qaharé ghazab jab koī ham sā na huā
phir ghalat kyā hai ki ham sā koī paidā na huā

Who could bear
And withstand
Her injustice
And her wrath?
Tell me then
If it's wrong
To lay a claim
That none was born
Ever like me.

*दरख़ुरे-क़हरे-ग़ज़ब*[1] *जब कोई हम-सा न हुआ*
*फिर ग़लत क्या है कि हम-सा कोई पैदा न हुआ*

---

*1. दुख और अन्याय को सह सकनेवाला*

بندگی میں بھی وہ آزادہ و خودبیں ہیں کہ ہم
اُلٹے پھر آئے، درِ کعبہ اگر وا نہ ہوا

bandagī méiñ bhī vō āẓād-o-ḳhudbīñ haiñ ki ham
ulṭé phir āé, daré-kābā agar vā na huā

Yes I serve
And I pray
Yet I am one
Who stands straight
And would not wait
What if it was
The Kaba's door
If it was closed.

*बन्दगी[1] में भी वो आज़ाद-ओ-ख़ुदबीं[2] हैं कि हम*
*उल्टे फिर आए, दरे-काबा[3] अगर वा[4] न हुआ*

---

*1. आराधना 2. मनमौजी तथा अभिमानी 3. काबे का दरवाज़ा 4. खुला*

سینے کا داغ ہے، وہ نالہ کہ لب تک نہ گیا
خاک کا رزق ہے، وہ قطرہ کہ دریا نہ ہوا

sīné kā dāgḥ hai, vo nālā ki lab tak na gayā
ḳhāk kā riẓḳ hai, vo qatrā ki dariyā na huā

Oh that grief and the pain
Which did not rise
To the lips and find
A voice, a cry
Lies festering in the heart
Like a drop of water
That did not find
Its way to the sea
But became mixed
With a handful of dust
And so got buried
In the earth.

*सीने का दाग़ है, वो नाला[1] कि लब तक न गया*
*ख़ाक का रिज़्क़[2] है, वो क़तरा[3] कि दरिया न हुआ*

---

*1. विलाप 2. अन्न 3. बूँद*

نام کا میرے ہے، جو دکھ کہ کسی کو نہ ملا
کام میں میرے ہے جو فتنہ کہ برپا نہ ہوا

nām kā méré hai, jo dukh ki kisī ko na milā
kām méiñ méré hai, jo ḟitnā ki barpā na huā

Who could have borne
The sadness and the grief
Which are my destiny?
Why is it
That it's only me
Whose no effort
Is accompanied
Without a crisis
And disaster?

*नाम का मेरे है, जो दुख कि किसी को न मिला*
*काम में मेरे है, जो फ़ित्ना[1] कि बरपा[2] न हुआ*

---

*1. उपद्रव 2. उपस्थित*

قطرے میں دجلہ دکھائی نہ دے اور جزو میں کل
کھیل لڑکوں کا ہوا دیدۂ بینا نہ ہوا

qataré méiñ dajlā dikhāī na dê aur juzv méiñ kul
khél laṛkoñ kā huā, dīda-é-bīnā na huā

If in a drop of water
One cannot see the river
Nor see the full
In the smallest part
What use is this eye?
It's but a toy
For a child to play
For only that eye
Is the real eye
Which can see
The whole in a part
Or the river
In a drop.

*क़तरे में दज़्ला[1] दिखाई न दे और जुज़्व[2] में कुल*
*खेल लड़कों का हुआ, दीद-ए-बीना[3] न हुआ*

---

*1. नदी का नाम 2. अंश 3. देखने वाली आंख*

جمع کرتے ہو کیوں رقیبوں کو
اِک تماشا ہوا گِلا نہ ہوا

jamā karté ho kyūñ raqībōñ ko
ik tamāshā huā gilā na huā

You are full of complaints
I know, oh I know
But why gather all my rivals
To make of it a show?

जमा करते हो क्यूं रक़ीबों[1] को
इक तमाशा हुआ गिला न हुआ

1. विरोधियों

ہم کہاں قسمت آزمانے جائیں
تو ہی جب خنجر آزما نہ ہوا

ham kahāñ qismat āẓmāné jāéñ
tū hī jab ḳhanjar-āẓmā na huā

Where do I go
What do I do
Now that even you
Have refused
To plunge your dagger
In my heart.

*हम कहां क़िस्मत आज़माने जाएं*
*तू ही जब ख़ंजर-आज़मा[1] न हुआ*

---

*1. ख़ंजर चलाने वाला*

کتنے شیریں ہیں تیرے لب کہ رقیب
گالیاں کھا کے بے مزا نہ ہوا

kitné shīrīñ haiñ téré lab ki raqīb
gāliyāñ khāké bémaẓā na huā

Oh the sweetness
Of your lips
That even
Words unkind
Thrown at the rival
Seem to him
To be words divine.

*कितने शीरीं[1] हैं तेरे लब कि रक़ीब*
*गालियां खाके बेमज़ा न हुआ*

---

*1. मीठे*

ہے خبر گرم اُن کے آنے کی
آج ہی گھر میں بوریا نہ ہوا

hai ḳhabar garm unké āné kī
āj hī ghar méīñ boriya na huā

That she will come
Today.
That is what
The rumours
Say.
But alas!
In the house
I be without
Even a mat
And that too
On this day.

*है ख़बर गर्म उनके आने की*
*आज ही घर में बोरिया[1] न हुआ*

---

*1. चटाई*

جان دی، دی ہوئی اُسی کی تھی
حق تو یوں ہے کہ حق ادا نہ ہوا

jān dī, dī huī usī kī thī
haq tō yūñ hai ki haq adā na huā

I gave my life
But this life
Was given by Him
And hence was His
Not mine.
So then
Where is the question
Of sacrifice?
And so the debt
Remains unpaid
Though I gave
My life
For Him.

*जान दी, दी हुई उसी की थी*
*हक़[1] तो यूं है कि हक़[2] अदा न हुआ*

---

*1. सच 2. फ़र्ज़*

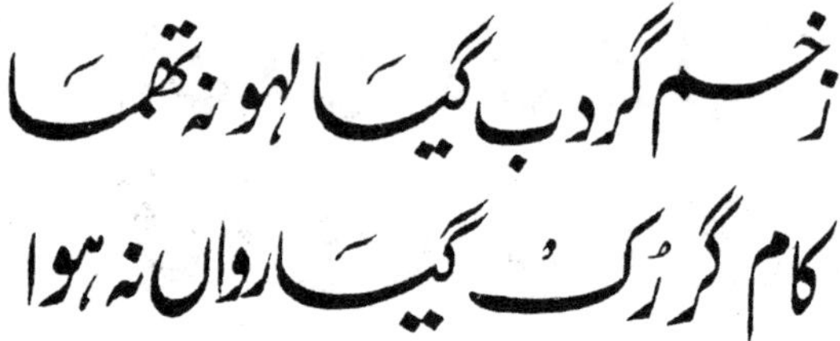

ẓaḳhm gar dab gayā lahū na thamā
kām gar ruk gayā ravāñ na huā

The wound seemed healed
Yet the blood continued to flow
But my work once stilled
Is stilled for good
And would not grow.

ज़ख़्म गर दब गया लहू न थमा
काम गर रुक गया रवां[1] न हुआ

---

1. शुरू होना

اعتبارِ عشق کی خانہ خرابی دیکھنا
غیر نے کی آہ لیکن وہ خفا مجھ پر ہوا

aitabāré-ishq kī ḳhānāḳharābī dékhnā
gḥair né kī āh lékin vo ḳhafā mujh par huā

Yes - she believes
Me to be
Her only love
But oh, the irony
Of it all
For even when
The other sighs
She doth feel
The blame
Is mine.

*ऐतबारे-इश्क़[1] की ख़ानाख़राबी[2] देखना*
*ग़ैर ने की आह लेकिन वो ख़फ़ा मुझ पर हुआ*

---

*1. प्रेम का विश्वास 2. बदक़िस्मती*

میں نے چاہا تھا کہ اندوہِ وفا سے چھوٹوں
وہ ستمگر مرے مرنے پہ بھی راضی نہ ہوا

maiñé chāhā thā ki andohé-vafā sé chhūtūñ
vo sitamgar méré marné pé bhī rāẓī na huā

Oh how I wished
That I could die
Only to be free
From the problem
And the bother
Of her fidelity.
But the cruel one
That she was
She would not agree
Even to that desire of mine
That I should die.

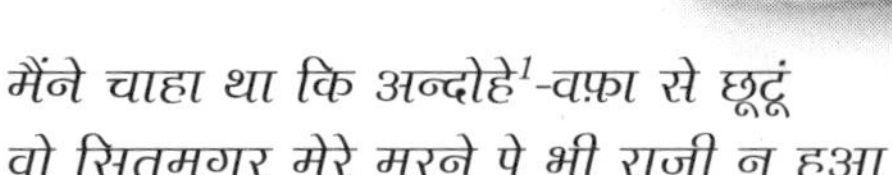
*मैंने चाहा था कि अन्दोहे[1]-वफ़ा से छूटूं*
*वो सितमगर मेरे मरने पे भी राज़ी न हुआ*

---

*1. मुसीबत*

ہے ایک تیر جس میں دونوں چھدے پڑے ہیں
وہ دن گئے کہ اپنا دل سے جگر جدا تھا

hai ék tīr jisméiñ dono chhidé paṛé haiñ
vo din gaé ki apnā dil sé jigar judā thā

The liver and the heart
Were once apart
But gone are those days.
For now
Both stand pierced
By the arrow
Shot by her.

है एक तीर जिसमें दोनों छिदे पड़े हैं
वो दिन गए कि अपना दिल से जिगर जुदा था

تھا خواب میں خیال کو تجھ سے معاملہ
جب آنکھ کھل گئی، نہ زیاں تھا، نہ سود تھا

thā k̤hvāb méiñ k̤hyāl ko tujhsé muāmalā
jab āñkh khul gai, na ẕiyāñ thā, na sūd thā

With you I had
An exchange of trade
But only in
One of my dreams.
And when
I woke
I found
There was
Neither gain
Nor loss
In the exchange.

*था ख़्वाब में ख़्याल को तुझसे मुआमला*
*जब आंख खुल गई, न ज़ियां[1] था, न सूद[2] था*

---

*1. हानि 2. लाभ*

ڈھانپا کفن نے داغِ عیوبِ برہنگی
میں، ورنہ ہر لباس میں ننگِ وجود تھا

ḍhāñpā kafan né dāghé-ayūbé barhanagī
maiñ, varnā har libās méiñ nangé-vajūd thā

No raiment can hide
The nakedness of life.
It's only the shroud
Which will cloud
All signs of my vice.

*ढांपा कफ़न ने दाग़े-अयूबे-बरहनगी[1]*
*मैं, वर्ना हर लिबास में नंगे-वजूद[2] था*

---

1. नंगापन 2. अस्तित्व पर शर्मिन्दा

اب میں ہوں اور ماتمِ یک شہر آرزو
توڑا جو تو نے آئینہ تمثال دار تھا

ab maiñ hūñ aur mātamé yak shahar ārẓū
tōṛā jo tūné āīnā timsāldār thā

This heart of mine
Is to me like
A city and a mirror
Of a myriad desires.
Now that you have broken
This mirror of mine
I am left to pine
For this city of mine
Of a myriad desires
And this heart of mine.

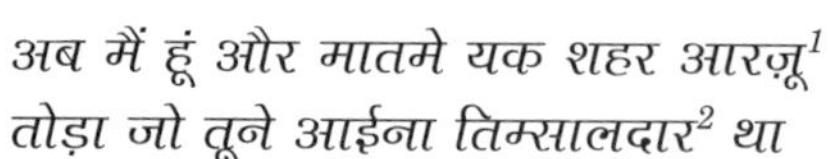
अब मैं हूं और मातमे यक शहर आरज़ू[1]
तोड़ा जो तूने आईना तिम्सालदार[2] था

---

1. कामना 2. मूर्तिकार/ चित्रकार

قید میں ہے ترے وحشی کو وہی زلف کی یاد
ہاں کچھ اک رنج گراں باریٔ زنجیر بھی تھا

qaid méiñ hai téré vahashī ko vahī ẓulf̣ kī yād
hāñ kuchh ik ranjé-garāñ bāri-é-ẓanjīr bhī thā

Oh! the grief and the burden
Of the life in the prison.
The weight of the chains
Grows all the more
When I recall
Your tresses flowing wild and free.

*क़ैद में है तेरे वहशी[1] को वही ज़ुल्फ़ की याद*
*हां कुछ इक रंजे-गरां बारि-ए-ज़ंजीर[2] भी था*

---

*1. पागल 2. ज़ंजीर के बोझ का कष्ट*

ریختے کے تمہیں استاد نہیں ہو غالبؔ
کہتے ہیں اگلے زمانے میں کوئی میرؔ بھی تھا

réḳhté ké tumhiñ ustād nahīñ ho 'Ġhālib'
kahté haiñ agalé ẓamāné méiñ koi 'Mīr' bhī thā

A master of Urdu verse
O Ghalib
You are not the only one
For they say
In earlier times
There was one
By the name of Meer.

*रेख़्ते[1] के तुम्हीं उस्ताद नहीं हो 'ग़ालिब'*
*कहते हैं अगले ज़माने में कोई 'मीर' भी था*

---

*1. उर्दू का पुराना नाम*

عرضِ نیازِ عشق کے قابل نہیں رہا
جس دل پہ ناز تھا مجھے وہ دل نہیں رہا

arẓé-niyāẓé-ishq ké qābil nahīñ rahā
jis dil pé nāẓ thā mujhé vo dil nahīñ rahā

There was a time
When this heart of mine
Made me proud
But now
It has changed
And become estranged
And so I find
I cannot avoid
My love
For her.

*अर्ज़े-नियाज़े-इश्क़[1] के क़ाबिल नहीं रहा*
*जिस दिल पे नाज़ था मुझे वो दिल नहीं रहा*

---

*1. प्रेम की अभिव्यक्ति*

جاتا ہوں داغِ حسرتِ ہستی لیے ہوئے
ہوں شمع کشتہ، درخورِ محفل نہیں رہا

jātā hūñ dāg̣hé hasraté hastī liyé hué
hūñ shamā-é-kushtā, darḳhuré-méhf̣il nahīñ rahā

Like a candle
Burnt out
I go out
Of this world
Bearing the scars
Of a grief-stricken heart
Of desires unfulfilled
Of hopes belied.

जाता हूं दाग़े-हसरते-हस्ती[1] लिए हुए
हूं शमा-ए-कुश्ता[2], दरख़ुरे-महफ़िल[3] नहीं रहा

---

*1. अधूरी इच्छाओं का जीवन 2. बुझा हुआ चिराग 3. सभा के योग्य*

مرنے کی اے دل! اور ہی تدبیر کر کہ میں
شایانِ دست و بازوئے قاتل نہیں رہا

marné kī ai dil aur hī tadbīr kar ki maiñ
shāyāné-dastō-bāẓū-é-qatil nahīñ rahā

Tell me O heart
Another way
Whereby to die
For now even she
Who should have slain me
Finds me not worthy
Of her dagger and strike.

*मरने की ऐ दिल और ही तदबीर[1] कर कि मैं*
*शायाने-दस्तो-बाज़ु-ए-क़ातिल[2] नहीं रहा*

---

1. उपाय 2. हत्यारे के हाथ के योग्य

وا کر دیے ہیں شوق نے بندِ نقابِ حُسن
غیر از نگاہ، اب کوئی حائل نہیں رہا

vā kar diyé haiñ shauq né bandé-naqābé-husn
ghair az nigāh, ab koī hāil nahīñ rahā

My longing and love
Have loosened and untied
Every string
That holds the veil
In its place.
Now it's only my eyes
Which bar the way
For that sight of her
The sight divine.

*वा[1] कर दिए हैं शौक़ ने बंदे-नक़ाबे-हुस्न[2]*
*ग़ैर अज़ निगाह[3], अब कोई हाइल[4] नहीं रहा*

---

*1. खुला हुआ 2. सुंदरता के नकाब की गिरह 3. दृष्टि के सिवा 4. बाधक*

عِشق سے طبیعت نے زیست کا مزا پایا
درد کی دوا پائی ، دردِ بے دوا پایا

ishq sé tabīyat né ẓīst kā maẓā pāyā
dard kī davā pāī, dard-bé-davā pāyā

It's love
Which has made
This life
Full of pleasures
And full of joy
And has given
For all its pain
A balm and a cure
And given a pain
For which there is
No balm no cure.

*इश्क़ से तबीअत ने ज़ीस्त[1] का मज़ा पाया*
*दर्द की दवा पाई, दर्द-बे-दवा पाया*

---

*1. ज़िन्दगी*

دوست دارِ دشمن ہے، اعتمادِ دل معلوم
آہ بے اثر دیکھی، نالہ نارسا پایا

dostdāré-dushman hai, aitamādé-dil mālūm
āh béasar dékhī, nālā nārsā pāyā

Who can trust this heart
It has become an ally
Of one
Who is the enemy.
And so no sigh
Nor lament
Will affect
And fruitless will be
Any complaint.

*दोस्तदारे-दुश्मन[1] है, एतमादे-दिल[2] मालूम*
*आह बेअसर देखी, नाला[3] नारसा[4] पाया*

---

*1. दुश्मन का दोस्त 2. दिल का सहारा 3. विलाप 4. जिसका असर न हो*

سادگی و پُرکاری، بے خودی و ہشیاری
حُسن کو تغافل میں جرأت آزما پایا

sādgī-o-purkārī, békḥudī-o-hushiyārī
husn ko tagḥafụl méiñ jurrat-āẓmāñ pāyā

At times so simple
At times so clever
At times so indifferent
And thus she plays
The great deceiver
But I must bear it all
For it is but a trial
Of my patience
And my love.

सादगी-ओ-पुरकारी[1], बेख़ुदी[2]-ओ-हुशियारी
हुस्न को तग़ाफ़ुल[3] में जुरअत-आज़मा[4] पाया

---

*1. चालाकी 2. बेहोशी 3. अचेतन 4. साहस से टकराने वाला*

ہوس کو ہے نشاطِ کار کیا کیا
نہ ہو مرنا، تو جینے کا مزا کیا

havas ko hai nishātė-kār kyā-kyā
na ho marnā, tō jīné kā maẓā kyā

It is the desire
The boundless desire
The want and the greed
That prods man
To action indeed.
If in this life
There was no death
What then would be the charm
In living and in life?

*हवस[1] को है निशाते-कार[2] क्या-क्या*
*न हो मरना, तो जीने का मज़ा क्या*

---

*1. लालच 2. काम करने की उमंग*

تجاہل پیشگی سے مدّعا کیا
کہاں تک اے سراپا ناز کیا، کیا

tajāhul péshgī sé mudaā kyā
kahāñ tak ai sarāpā nāẓ kyā-kyā

I know you know
And yet you show
You do not know
And you ask
What is it I say
And what is it I mean
When all the while
I know you know
What I say
And what I mean.

*तजाहुल[1] पेशगी[2] से मुद्दआ[3] क्या*
*कहां तक ऐ सरापा-नाज़[4] क्या-क्या*

---

*1. जान-बूझ कर अनजान बनना 2. पहले से 3. मामला 4. सर से पांव तक घमंडी*

نفس، موجِ محیطِ بےخودی ہے
تغافل ہائے ساقی کا گِلا کیا

nafas, maujé-muhīté-békhudī hai
taghāful-hāé-sāqī kā gilā kyā

Every breath I take
Is like a wave
In the sea
Of ecstasy.
So what if
The Saqi
Is so ungenerous
And so indifferent
What reason is there
For me to complain?

*नफ़स[1], मौजे-मुहीते-बेख़ुदी[2] है*
*तग़ाफ़ुल-हाए-साक़ी[3] का गिला क्या*

---

*1. सांस 2. बेहोशी से घिरा हुआ 3. साक़ी की उपेक्षा*

دلِ ہر قطرہ، ہے سازِ انا البحر
ہم اُس کے ہیں ہمارا پوچھنا کیا

dilé-har-qatrā, hai sāz̤é-analbahr
ham uské haiñ hamārā puchhanā kyā

Every drop
Sings and sees
Itself as a part
Of the boundless sea.
Then why ask
Who am I
When I really am
A note
In the music of
Eternity.

दिले-हर-क़तरा[1], है साज़े-अनलबहर[2]
हम उसके हैं हमारा पूछना क्या

---

1 बूंद 2. समुद्र का संगीत

بلائے جاں ہے غالبؔ اُس کی ہر بات
عبارت کیا، اشارت کیا، ادا کیا

balā-é-jāñ hai 'Ghālib' uskī har bāt
ibārat kyā, ishārat kyā, adā kyā

Her every look
Her every glance
Her every word
Her every stance
Is O Ghalib
One that kills
And takes my life
Away.

*बला-ए-जां है 'ग़ालिब' उसकी हर बात*
*इबारत[1] क्या, इशारत[2] क्या, अदा क्या*

---

*1. लेख 2. संकेत*

دوست غمخواری میں میری، سعی فرمائیں گے کیا
زخم کے بھرنے تلک، ناخن نہ بڑھ جائیں گے کیا

dost g̣hamḳhvārī méiñ mérī, saī f̣armāéñgé kyā
ẓaḳhm ké bharné talak, nāḳhun na baḍh jāéñgé kyā

My friends
Who soothe
And heal
My wounds
But I know
Oh I know
By the time
The wounds will heal
Their pared nails
Again will grow.

*दोस्त ग़मख़्वारी[1] में मेरी, सई[2] फ़रमाएंगे क्या*
*ज़ख़्म के भरने तलक, नाख़ुन न बढ़ जाएंगे क्या*

---

*1. सहानुभूति 2. सहायता*

بے نیازی حد سے گزری، بندہ پرور کب تلک
ہم کہیں گے حالِ دل، اور آپ فرمائیں گے کیا

béniyāẓī hadh sé guẓrī, bandāparvar kab talak
ham kahéñgé hālé-dil, aur āp ḟarmāéñgé kyā

For how long
Oh but for how long
Will she remain
Immune
To all my pleas
And all my woes?
And for how long
Will I continue
To voice my ills
And she continue
To ask me thus
Yes, what is it
Oh, What is it?

*बेनियाज़ी[1] हद से गुज़री, बन्दापरवर कब तलक*
*हम कहेंगे हाले-दिल, और आप फ़रमाएंगे क्या*

---

*1. निस्पृहता*

حضرتِ ناصح گر آویں، دیدہ و دل فرشِ راہ
کوئی مجھ کو یہ تو سمجھا دو کہ سمجھائیں گے کیا

haẓraté-nāséh gar āvéñ, dida-o-dil ṭarsh-é-rāh
koī mujhko yé tō samjhā do ki samajhāéñgé kyā

He is welcome
The respected preacher
I'll roll out the carpet
In his welcome.
But will someone
Tell me and explain
What after all
To me
He'll explain?

हज़रते-नासेह[1] गर आवें, दीद-ओ-दिल फ़र्श-ए-राह[2]
कोई मुझको ये तो समझा दो कि समझाएंगे क्या

1. उपदेशक 2. पलकों को स्वागत में बिछाना

آج واں تیغ و کفن باندھے ہوئے جاتا ہوں میں
عذر میرے قتل کرنے میں وہ اب لائیں گے کیا

āj vāñ tégḥ-o-kaf̣an bāndhé hué jātā hūñ maiñ
uẓr méré qatl karné méiñ vo ab lāéñgé kyā

With my sword
And with my shroud
I will go
And find out
The reason she gives
For slaying me not
Today.

*आज वां तेग़[1]-ओ-कफ़न बांधे हुए जाता हूं मैं*
*उज़्र[2] मेरे क़त्ल करने में वो अब लाएंगे क्या*

---

*1. तलवार 2. बहाना*

خانہ زادِ زلف ہیں، زنجیر سے بھاگیں گے کیوں
ہیں گرفتارِ وفا، زنداں سے گھبرائیں گے کیا

kḥānāẓādé-ẓulf̣ haiñ, ẓanjīr sé bhāgéñgé kyūñ
haiñ girif̣tār-é-vaf̣a, ẓindāñ sé ghabrāéñgé kyā

When once caught
And made a slave
By love's flowing hair.
Why then fear
The prison bars
And run from
The weight of the chains?

*ख़ानाज़ादे-ज़ुल्फ़[1] हैं, ज़ंजीर से भागेंगे क्यूं*
*हैं गिरिफ़्तारे-वफ़ा, ज़िन्दां[2] से घबराएंगे क्या*

---

*1. ज़ुल्फ़ों का क़ैदी 2. जेल*

رات دن گردش میں ہیں سات آسماں
ہو رہے گا کچھ نہ کچھ گھبرائیں کیا

rāt din gardish méiñ haiñ sāt āsmāñ
ho rahégā kuchh na kuchh ghabrāéñ kyā

Day and night
Without a pause
The seven skies
Revolve.
Why worry then
For something will happen
If not this
Then surely that.

*रात दिन गर्दिश[1] में हैं सात आसमां*
*हो रहेगा कुछ न कुछ घबराएं क्या*

---

*1.* घूम रहे हैं

پوچھتے ہیں وہ کہ غالبؔ کون ہے
کوئی بتلاؤ کہ ہم بتلائیں کیا

pūchhté haiñ vo ki 'Ġhālib' kaun hai
koi batlāo ki ham batlāéñ kyā

She asks
Who after all
Is Ghalib.
Will someone tell me
What
I can tell
In reply?

*पूछते हैं वो कि 'ग़ालिब' कौन है*
*कोई बतलाओ कि हम बतलाएं क्या*

شمع بجھتی ہے تو اس میں سے دھواں اٹھتا ہے
شعلۂ عشق سیہ پوش ہوا میرے بعد

shamaā bujhtī hai tō usméiñ sé dhuāñ uṭhtā hai
sholā-é-ishq siyāhposh huā méré bād

The black smoke
Is all that remains
Of the dying flame.
And so
When I'm gone
All that will remain
Is the black cloak
Over
Love's bright flame.

*शमआ बुझती है तो उसमें से धुआं उठता है*
*शोला-ए-इश्क़ सियाहपोश[1] हुआ मेरे बाद*

---

*1. बिल्कुल काला*

کیوں جل گیا نہ تابِ رُخِ یار دیکھ کر
جلتا ہوں اپنی طاقتِ دیدار دیکھ کر

kyūñ jal gayā na tābé-ruḳhé yār dékh kar
jaltā hūñ apnī tāqaté-dīdār dékh kar

Her beauty
Is bright like fire
And yet I was not burnt.
For there must have been
That strength in me
Which makes me burn
With jealousy
At my own intensity
Of seeing her beauty
And yet not burn.

क्यों जल गया न ताबे-रुख़े[1] यार देख कर
जलता हूं अपनी ताक़ते-दीदार[2] देख कर

---

1. प्रेमिका के चेहरे की चमक 2. देखने की शक्ति

آتا ہے میرے قتل کو پُرجوشِ رشک سے
مرتا ہوں اُس کے ہاتھ میں تلوار دیکھ کر

ātā hai méré qatl ko, purjoshé rashk sé
martā hūñ uské hāth méiñ talwār dékh kar

How lucky the sword
She holds in her hand
Why then should she harbour
Against me the desire
To have me slain?
When as it is
I die of envy
For the sword
She holds in her hand.

आता है मेरे क़त्ल को, पुरजोशे-रश्क[1] से
मरता हूं उसके हाथ में तलवार देख कर

---

1. ईर्ष्या से भरा आवेश

واحسرتا کہ یار نے کھینچا ستم سے ہاتھ
ہم کو حریصِ لذتِ آزار دیکھ کر

vā hasratā ki yār né khéñchā sitam sé hāth
hamko harīsé-laẕẕaté-āẕār dékh kar

Alas she came to know
That I enjoy
The tortures she inflicts
And the pain she gives.
And so she has
Withdrawn
Her hand
And left me alone.

*वा हसरता[1] कि यार ने खेंचा सितम से हाथ*
*हमको हरीसे[2]-लज़्ज़ते-आज़ार[3] देख कर*

---

*1. अफ़सोस 2. लालायित 3. दुख का स्वाद*

یارب! نہ وہ سمجھے ہیں نہ سمجھیں گے مری بات
دے اور دل اُن کو جو نہ دے مجھ کو زباں اور

yā Rab! na vo samajhé haiñ na samajhéñgé mérī bāt
dé aur dil unko jo na dé mujhko ẓubāñ aur

She has not understood
Nor will she understand
Hence O God
I pray
If not to me
Another tongue
Then do give her
Another heart
So she can understand
All I wish to say.

या रब! न वो समझे हैं न समझेंगे मेरी बात
दे और दिल उनको जो न दे मुझको ज़ुबां और

ہرچند سُبک دست ہوئے بُت شِکنی میں
ہم ہیں، تو ابھی راہ میں ہے سنگِ گراں اور

harchand subukdast hué butshikanī méiñ
ham haiñ, tō abhī rāh méiñ hai sangé-girāñ aur

Indeed I excel
In idol break
But Oh for that stone
That heavy stone
That lies in the way.

*हरचन्द सुबुकदस्त[1] हुए बुतशिकनी[2] में*
*हम हैं, तो अभी राह में है संगे-गिरां[3] और*

---

*1. दक्ष/ कुशल 2. मूर्ति तोड़ना 3. भारी पत्थर*

پاتے نہیں جب راہ تو چڑھ جاتے ہیں نالے
رکتی ہے مری طبع، تو ہوتی ہے رواں اور

pāté nahīñ jab rāh tō chaḍh jāté haiñ nālé
ruktī mérī hai tabaā, tō hotī hai ravāñ aur

Confined by its banks
And finding no way
For its outpour
The river overflows
And breaks its banks.
Thus my sorrow
Overflows
And like the river
Breaks its banks.

पाते नहीं जब राह तो चढ़ जाते हैं नाले
रुकती मेरी है तबआ[1], तो होती है रवां[2] और

---

1. मिज़ाज 2. गतिशील

ہیں اور بھی دنیا میں سخنور بہت اچھے
کہتے ہیں کہ غالبؔ کا ہے اندازِ بیاں اور

haiñ aur bhī duniyā méiñ sukhanvar bahut achhé
kahté haiñ ki 'Ghālib' kā hai andāzé-bayāñ aur

There are in the world
Poets who are great.
But they say
There was that Ghalib
Who could say
As nobody could
And nobody can.

*हैं और भी दुनिया में सुख़नवर[1] बहुत अच्छे*
*कहते हैं कि 'ग़ालिब' का है अंदाज़े-बयां और*

---

*1. शायर*

جاتے ہوئے کہتے ہو قیامت کو ملیں گے
کیا خوب قیامت کا ہے گویا کوئی دن اور

jāté hué kahté ho qayāmat ko milẽñgé
kyā ḳhub qayāmat kā hai goyā koī din aur

We'll meet again
On judgement day
That's what you said
While going away.
My God!
As if there was
Another judgement day
Than the day
You went away.

जाते हुए कहते हो क़यामत को मिलेंगे
क्या ख़ूब क़यामत का है गोया कोई दिन और

نہ گلِ نغمہ ہوں نہ پردۂ ساز
میں ہوں اپنی شکست کی آواز

na gulé-naghmā hūñ, na parda-é-sāz
maiñ hūñ apnī shikast kī āvāz

I am not
The sweet song
That blossoms.
I am not
The sweet note
In the melody.
I am only
The piteous sound
Of my own defeat
Of my own fall.

*न गुले-नग़्मा[1] हुं, न पर्दे-ए-साज़[2]*
*मैं हूं अपनी शिकस्त की आवाज़*

---

*1. फूलों की सरसराहट 2. संगीत का साज़*

تو، اور آرائشِ خمِ کاکل
میں، اور اندیشہ ہائے دور و دراز

tū aur, ārāishé-ḳhamé-kākul
maiñ aur, andéshāhāé dūr-o-darāẓ

While you are busy
Arranging your curls
I am far
And full of fear.

तू और, आराइशे-ख़मे-काकुल[1]
मैं और, अन्देशाहाए[2] दूर-ओ-दराज़

---

1. बल खाए हुए बालों की सजावट 2. शंकाएं

ہوں گرفتارِ اُلفتِ صیّاد
ورنہ باقی ہے طاقتِ پرواز

hūñ giriftār-é-ulfaté-sayyād
varnā bāqī hai tāqaté-parvāz

I could also take wing
Yet I remain
Enslaved by
The love
For the hunter.

हूं गिरिफ़्तारे-उल्फ़ते-सय्याद[1]
वर्ना बाक़ी है ताक़ते-परवाज़[2]

---

1. शिकारी के प्रेम में गिरफ़्तार 2. उड़ने की शक्ति

دہنِ شیر میں جا بیٹھئے لیکن اے دل
نہ کھڑے ہوجیے خوبانِ دل آزار کے پاس

dahné-shér méiñ jā baiṭhiyé lékin ai dil
na khaṛé hūjiyé ḳhūbāné-dil-āẓār ké pās

Oh my heart!
Better it is
To dwell in the mouth
Of the dreaded lion
Rather than stand
Beside the beloved
Fair and of beauty
But who
Has the power
To torment me so.

*दहने-शेर[1] में जा बैठिए लेकिन ऐ दिल*
*न खड़े हूजिए ख़ूबाने-दिल-आज़ार[2] के पास*

---

*1.* शेर के मुंह *2.* दिल को चोट पहुंचाने वाली सुंदरियां

عاشقی صبر طلب اور تمنّا بے تاب
دل کا کیا رنگ کروں خونِ جگر ہونے تک

āshiqī sabr-talab aur tamannā bétāb
dil kā kyā rang karūñ ḳhūné-jigar honé tak

Love demands patience
But the desires make one
So impatient.
Indeed what do I do
With this restless heart
Till it is soaked
With blood, red blood?

*आशिक़ी सब्र-तलब[1] और तमन्ना बेताब[2]*
*दिल का क्या रंग करूं ख़ूने-जिगर होने तक*

---

*1. आशिक़ी धैर्य चाहती है 2. अधीर, व्याकुल*

ہم نے مانا کہ تغافل نہ کروگے، لیکن
خاک ہو جائیں گے ہم تم کو خبر ہونے تک

hamné mānā ki taghāful na karogé, lékin
ḳhāk ho jāéñgé ham tum ko ḳhabar honé tak

You will never ignore
Or be indifferent to me
This I agree.
But by the time
You come to hear
Of me
I will have turned
To dust
For all to see.

*हमने माना कि तग़ाफ़ुल[1] न करोगे, लेकिन*
*ख़ाक हो जाएंगे हम तुमको ख़बर होने तक*

---

*1. लापरवाही*

پرتوِ خور سے ہے شبنم کو فنا کی تعلیم
میں بھی ہوں ایک عنایت کی نظر ہونے تک

partavé-ķhūr sé hai shabnam ko ṭanā kī tālīm
maiñ bhī hūñ ék ināyat kī nazar honé tak

The dew does die
At a glance from the sun.
I too survive
Only as long
That I receive
A glance from her.

परतवे-ख़ूर[1] से है शबनम को फ़ना की तालीम[2]
मैं भी हूं एक इनायत[3] की नज़र होने तक

---

1. सूर्य की किरण 2. मर मिटने की शिक्षा 3. कृपा

غمِ ہستی کا اسدؔ کس سے ہو جز مرگ علاج
شمع ہر رنگ میں جلتی ہے سحر ہونے تک

ghamé-hastī kā 'Asad' kisasé ho juẓ marg ilāj
shamaā har rang méiñ jaltī hai sahar honé tak

Only death can end
The pain of the moth
Playing with the flame.
And yet the flame
Must burn on
In all its colour
Till the dawn.

*ग़मे-हस्ती का 'असद' किससे हो जुज़[1] मर्ग[2] इलाज*
*शमआ हर रंग में जलती है सहर[3] होने तक*

---

*1. जीवन का दुख 2. सिवाय मौत 3. प्रातःकाल*

تیرے ہی جلوے کا ہے یہ دھوکا کہ آج تک
بے اختیار دوڑے ہے گل در قفائے گل

téré hī jalvé kā hai yé dhokā ki āj tak
béikḥtiyār dauṛé hai gulo-dar-qafā-é-gul

Deceived by your beauty
Rose after rose
Blooms and pursues
One after the other
In eager
Chase.

*तेरे ही जल्वे का है ये धोका कि आज तक*
*बेइख़्तियार दौड़े है गुलो-दर-क़फ़ा-ए-गुल*[1]

---

*1. फूल के पीछे फूल*

مجھ کو دیارِ غیر میں مارا وطن سے دور
رکھ لی مرے خدا نے مری بےکسی کی شرم

mujhko dayāré-gḥair méiñ mārā vatan sé dūr
rakh lī méré ḳhudā né mérī békasī kī sharm

Oh for a death
In a foreign land
Far from a country
That's my own.
And so has God
Saved me from disgrace
Of my own
Helplessness.

मुझको दयारे-ग़ैर[1] में मारा वतन से दूर
रख ली मेरे ख़ुदा ने मेरी बेकसी की शर्म

---

1. पराए घर

وہ فراق اور وہ وصال کہاں
وہ شب و روز و ماہ و سال کہاں

vo ḟirāq aur vo visāl kahāñ
vo shabo-rōẓō-māho-sāl kahāñ

Oh where are those days
The months and years
With all their memories
Of union and separation?

*वो फ़िराक़[1] और वो विसाल[2] कहां*
*वो शबो-रोज़ो-माहो-साल[3] कहां*

---

*1. वियोग 2. मिलन 3. रात, दिन, महीने और साल*

فرصتِ کار و بارِ شوق کِسے
ذوقِ نظّارۂ جمال کہاں

fursaté-kārobāré shauq kisé
zauqé-nazzārā-é-jamāl kahāñ

Who has the time
For this business of love?
And who has the desire
To constantly admire
Beauty
Even if it is
In all its glory?

फ़ुर्सते-कारोबारे शौक़ किसे
ज़ौक़े-नज़्ज़ारा-ए-जमाल[1] कहां

---

1. सुंदरता देखने की चाह

تھی وہ اِک شخص کے تصور سے
اب وہ رعنائیِ خیال کہاں

thī vo ik shaḳhs ké tasavvur sé
ab vo rānāi-é-ḳhyāl kahāñ

All my thought
Was full of beauty
For behind it all
Was your beauty.
Now with that beauty gone
So have my thoughts
Who knows indeed
Where both have gone?

*थी वो इक शख़्स[1] के तसव्वुर[2] से*
*अब वो रानाई-ए-ख़्याल[3] कहां*

---

*1. व्यक्ति 2. कल्पना 3. सौंदर्य की कल्पना*

فکرِ دنیا میں سر کھپاتا ہوں
میں کہاں اور یہ وبال کہاں

f̣ikré-duniyā méiñ sar khapātā hūñ
maiñ kahāñ aur yé vabāl kahāñ

Needless do I worry
And break my head
Over the problems
Of this world.
Indeed what for do I
And why should I
Break my head
Over all these problems
And all these cares?

*फ़िक्रे-दुनिया में सर खपाता हूं*
*मैं कहां और ये वबाल कहां*

ہم سے کھل جاؤ بوقتِ مے پرستی ایک دن
ورنہ ہم چھیڑیں گے رکھ کے عذرِ مستی ایک دن

hamsé khul jāo bavaqté-maiy-parastī ék din
varnā ham chhéṛéñgé rakhkar uẓré-mastī ék din

Just once
Oh just once
Come share the cup
And abandon behind
All modesty.
Or else
There will be time
When I shall take liberties
And blame it all
On inebriety.

*हमसे खुल जाओ बवक़्ते-मय-परस्ती[1] एक दिन*
*वर्ना हम छेड़ेंगे रखकर उज़्रे-मस्ती[2] एक दिन*

---

*1. मदिरा पीते समय 2. मस्ती का बहाना*

دیر نہیں، حرم نہیں، در نہیں، آستاں نہیں
بیٹھے ہیں رہ گزر پہ ہم، غیر ہمیں اٹھائے کیوں

dair nahīñ, haram nahīñ, dar nahīñ, āstāñ nahīñ
baiṭhé haiñ rahguẓar pa ham, g̣hair hamén̄ uṭhāé kyūñ

Not for me
The sanctuaries and shrine
Not for me
The palaces fine
I just lie
By the wayside.
Still why is it
I am not left
In peace
And from here too
I be removed?

*दैर[1] नहीं, हरम[2] नहीं, दर नहीं, आस्तां[3] नहीं*
*बैठे हैं रहगुज़र प[4] हम, ग़ैर हमें उठाए क्यूं*

---

*1. मंदिर 2. काबा 3. चौखट 4. सड़क पर*

قیدِ حیات و بندِ غم، اصل میں دونوں ایک ہیں
موت سے پہلے آدمی غم سے نجات پائے کیوں

qaidé-hayāt-o-bandé-g̣ham, asl méiñ dono ék haiñ
maut sé pahlé ādamī g̣ham sé nijāt pāé kyūñ

The fetters of sorrow
Are one
Like the prison
Of life.
Why then
Should this
Pain and grief
Cease
Before we shed
The mortal coil?

*क़ैदे-हयात-ओ-बन्दे-ग़म*[1]*, अस्ल में दोनों एक हैं*
*मौत से पहले आदमी ग़म से निजात*[2] *पाए क्यूं*

---

*1. जीवन और दुख का बंधन 2. रिहाई*

غالبِ خستہ کے بغیر کون سے کام بند ہیں
روئیے زار زار کیا، کیجیے ہائے ہائے کیوں

'Ģhālib'-é-ķhastā ké bagḥair kaun sé kām band haiñ
rōiyé ẓār ẓār kyā, kījiyé hāé hāé kyūñ

What in the world
Would stop
When Ghalib
Is gone?
Then why
This weeping
And why
This mourning?

'ग़ालिबे'-ख़स्ता[1] के बग़ैर कौन से काम बन्द हैं
रोइए ज़ार-ज़ार[2] क्या, कीजिए हाय-हाय क्यूं

1. दुर्दशा ग्रस्त ग़ालिब 2. फूट-फूट कर

ملتی ہے خوئے یار سے نار، التہاب میں
کافر ہوں، گر نہ ملتی ہو راحت عذاب میں

miltī hai ḳhū-é-yār sé nār, iltihāb méiñ
kāf̣ir hūñ, gar na miltī ho rāhat aẓāb méiñ

Her nature, her ire
Is indeed like fire.
Consider me a kafir
If I say I do not
Derive peace and comfort
In her ire
Which is like fire.

*मिलती है ख़ू-ए-यार[1] से नार[2], इल्तिहाब[3] में*
*काफ़िर हूं, गर न मिलती हो राहत अज़ाब[4] में*

---

*1. प्रेयसी का स्वभाव 2. नरक की आग 3. लपट 4. पीड़ा*

تا پھر نہ انتظار میں نیند آئے عمر بھر
آنے کا عہد کر گئے، آئے جو خواب میں

tā pḥir na intézār méiñ nīñd āé umr bhar
āné kā ahad kar gaé, āé jo ḳhvāb méiñ

Oh for the curse
Of sleepless nights
Which I shall bear
Forever through life
For she promised to come
In one of my dreams.

*ता फ़िर न इन्तज़ार में नींद आए उम्र भर*
*आने का अहद[1] कर गए, आए जो ख़्वाब में*

---

*1.* वादा

قاصد کے آتے آتے، خط اک اور لکھ رکھوں
میں جانتا ہوں، جو وہ لکھیں گے جواب میں

qāsid ké āté-āté, ḳhat ik aur likh rakhūñ
maiñ jāntā hūñ, jo vo likhéñgé javāb méiñ

I know her reply
To the letter I wrote
And so therefore
Even before
The courier arrives
Let me write
Another letter
In reply.

*क़ासिद[1] के आते-आते, ख़त इक और लिख रखूं*
*मैं जानता हूं, जो वो लिखेंगे जवाब में*

---

*1.* पत्रवाहक

مجھ تک کب اُن کی بزم میں آتا تھا دورِ جام
ساقی نے کچھ مِلا نہ دیا ہو شراب میں

mujh tak kab unkī baẓm méiñ ātā thā daur-é-jām
sāqī né kuchh milā na diyā ho sharāb méiñ

When Oh When
Did the cup
Ever come
To me?
And today if it's come
Then probably
The saqi
Has mixed something
In the cup of wine
That she has brought
To me.

*मुझ तक कब उनकी बज़्म में*[1] *आता था दौर-ए-जाम*
*साक़ी ने कुछ मिला न दिया हो शराब में*

---

*1. सभा में*

میں مضطرب ہوں وصل میں خوفِ رقیب سے
ڈالا ہے تم کو وہم نے کس پیچ و تاب میں

maiñ muẓtarib hūñ vasl méiñ ķhauf̣é-raqīb sé
ḍālā hai tumko vaham né kis pécho-tāb méiñ

I am uneasy
Even in this hour
Of our meeting
For fear
The other
Will come
And disturb.
But pray
Let me know
What makes you so
Even in this hour
Of our meeting
So restless
And afraid?

मैं मुज़्तरिब[1] हूं वस्ल[2] में ख़ौफ़े-रक़ीब[3] से
डाला है तुमको वहम ने किस पेचो-ताब[4] में

1. बेचैन 2. मिलन 3. प्रेम में विरोधी का भय 4. आशंका

رو میں ہے رخشِ عمر کہاں دیکھیے تھمے
نے ہاتھ باگ پر ہے، نہ پا ہے رکاب میں

raū méiñ hai rakhshé-umr kahāñ dékhiyé thamé
na hāth bāg par hai, na pā hai rakāb méiñ

Whither life's steed
Galloping wild
Without control
On the feet or the reins?
Whither it will go
I know it not
Where it will stop
I know it not.

*रौ[1] में है रख़्शे-उम्र[2] कहां देखिए थमे*
*न हाथ बाग[3] पर है, न पा है रकाब में*

---

*1. तीव्र गति 2. आयु का घोड़ा 3. लगाम*

یاد تھیں ہم کو بھی رنگارنگ بزم آرائیاں
لیکن اب نقش و نگارِ طاقِ نسیاں ہو گئیں

yād thī hamko bhī rangārang baẓm ārāiyāñ
lékin ab naq̇sho-nigāré-tāké-nisiyāñ hō gaīñ

How I recall
Those days
Of colour
And of pleasure.
But now alas
All that I see
Are flowers and designs
Adorning the shelves
Of the dusty past.

*याद थीं हमको भी रंगारंग बज़्म आराइयां*[1]
*लेकिन अब नक़्शो-निगारे*[2]*-ताक़े-निसियां*[3] *हो गईं*

---

*1. सभा की सजावट 2. बेल-बूटे 3. धुँधले अतीत का ताक़*

نیند اُس کی ہے، دماغ اُس کا ہے راتیں اُس کی ہیں
تیری زلفیں جس کے بازو پر پریشاں ہوگئیں

nīñd uskī hai, dimāgḥ uskā hai rātéñ uskī haiñ
térī ẓulféñ jiské bāẓū par paréshāñ ho gaīñ

His the sleep
And his the peace
His the night
And his the dreams
On whose arms
My love
Rest thy tresses
Wild and free.

*नींद उसकी है, दिमाग़ उसका है रातें उसकी हैं*
*तेरी ज़ुल्फ़ें जिसके बाज़ू पर परेशां हो गईं*

تم جانو تم کو غیر سے جو رسم و راہ ہو
مجھ کو بھی پوچھتے رہو تو کیا گناہ ہو

tum jāno tum ko gẖair sé jo rasmo-rāh ho
mujhko bhī pūchhté raho tō kyā gunāh ho

You know better
Your relations
With the other.
But would it be a crime
To spare some time.
And ask about me
About how I am
And where I am?

*तुम जानो तुमको ग़ैर से जो रस्मो-राह[1] हो*
*मुझको भी पूछते रहो तो क्या गुनाह हो*

---

*1.* संबंध

کیا وہ بھی بے گنہ کُش و حق ناشناس ہیں
مانا کہ تم بشر نہیں، خورشید و ماہ ہو

kyā vo bhī bégunāh kusho-haq nā shanās haiñ
mānā ki tum bashar nahiñ, ḳhurshīd-o-māh ho

Agreed you are
No mortal ordinary
But as powerful
As the sun and the moon.
But are they too
Heartless fiends
Alien to truth
And slayer
Of many?

क्या वो भी बेगुनाह कुशो[1]-हक़ ना शनास[2] हैं
माना कि तुम बशर[3] नहीं, ख़ुर्शीद-ओ-माह[4] हो

---

1. निर्दोष लोगों का वध करने वाला 2. सत्य को न जानने वाला
3. मानव 4. सूर्य और चन्द्रमा

موت کا ایک دن معیّن ہے
نیند کیوں رات بھر نہیں آتی

maut kā ék din muayyan hai
nīñd kyūñ rāt bhar nahīñ ātī

After all
Death will come
For certain it is
That for it
The day is fixed.
Then indeed
Why these
Restless nights
When sleep abandons
The sleepy eyes?

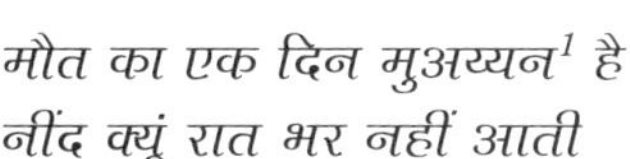

मौत का एक दिन मुअय्यन[1] है
नींद क्यूं रात भर नहीं आती

1. निश्चित

آگے آتی تھی حالِ دل پہ ہنسی
اب کِسی بات پر نہیں آتی

āgé ātī thī hālé-dil pé hañsī
ab kisī bāt par nahīñ ātī

Time was
When I laughed
And smiled
Even at my
Own state.
Now indeed
There's nothing
To make me
Laugh or
Smile.

आगे आती थी हाले-दिल पे हंसी
अब किसी बात पर नहीं आती

ہے کچھ ایسی ہی بات، جو چپ ہوں
ورنہ کیا بات کر نہیں آتی

hai kuchh aisī hī bāt, jo chup hūñ
varnā kyā bāt kar nahīñ ātī

There is something
Which compels me
To seal my tongue.
Otherwise
Do you think
I have no speech
Nor a tongue?

*है कुछ ऐसी ही बात, जो चुप हूं*
*वर्ना क्या बात कर नहीं आती*

ہم وہاں ہیں، جہاں سے ہم کو بھی
کچھ ہماری خبر نہیں آتی

ham vahāñ haiñ, jahāñ sé hamko bhī
kuchh hamārī ḳhabar nahīñ ātī

Oh I am lost
Some place
Somewhere
From which place
I have no news
Nor can hear
Even
About myself.

*हम वहां हैं, जहां से हमको भी*
*कुछ हमारी ख़बर नहीं आती*

واعظ نہ تم پیو ، نہ کسی کو پلا سکو
کیا بات ہے تمہاری شرابِ طہور کی

vāiẓ na tum piyo, na kisī ko pilā sako
kyā bāt hai tumhārī sharābé-tuhūr kī

You neither drink
Nor offer to others
Then O priest
Why should you speak
Of the wine
That's divine
Which no one can taste
And no one drink?

*वाइज़[1] न तुम पियो, न किसी को पिला सको*
*क्या बात है तुम्हारी शराबे-तुहूर[2] की*

---

*1. उपदेशक 2. जन्नत की मदिरा*

عمر ہرچند کہ ہے برق خرام
دل کے خوں کرنے کی فرصت ہی سہی

umr harchand ki hai barq ḳhirām
dil ké ḳhūñ karné kī fursat hī sahī

A flash of lightning
Is life.
Yet short as it is
There is time
To leave behind
A bleeding heart.

उम्र हरचन्द[1] कि है बर्क़-ख़िराम[2]
दिल के ख़ूं करने की फ़ुर्सत ही सही

1. यद्यपि 2. बिजली जैसी चाल

پھر اس انداز سے بہار آئی
کہ ہوئے مہر و مہ تماشائی

phir is andāẓ sé bahār āī
ki hué méhro-mah tamāshāī

Into spectators
Have turned
The moon and the sun
For spring has come
Again with glory
And all its splendour.

*फिर इस अन्दाज़ से बहार आई*
*कि हुए मेहरो-मह[1] तमाशाई*

---

*1.* सूर्य और चन्द्रमां

جب تک دہانِ زخم نہ پیدا کرے کوئی
مشکل کہ تجھ سے راہِ سخن وا کرے کوئی

jab tak dahāné-ẓaḳhm na paidā karé koī
mushkil ki tujhsé rāhé-sukhan vā karé koī

The wound
Needs a mouth
To pour out
All that's beneath.
And so do I
Need a wound
In my heart
To pour out
All my woes.

जब तक दहाने-ज़ख़्म न पैदा करे कोई
मुश्किल कि तुझसे राहे-सुख़न वा[1] करे कोई

---

1. बातचीत का मार्ग खोलना

عالم غبارِ وحشتِ مجنوں ہے سر بسر
کب تک خیالِ طرّۂ لیلا کرے کوئی

ālam gḥubāré-vahshaté-majnūñ hai sar-ba-sar
kab tak kḥyālé-turra-é-lailā karé koī

Surely it is
The dust
Raised by the madness
Of Majnu's love
That covers this world.
Otherwise
How long can one
Brood only on
Laila's grace
Her tresses
And her face?

*आलम[1] ग़ुबारे-वहशते-मजनूं[2] है सर-ब-सर[3]*
*कब तक ख़्याले-तुर्र-ए-लैला[4] करे कोई*

---

*1. संसार 2. मजनूं के पागलपन की धूल 3. बराबर 4. लैला की ज़ुल्फ़ की कल्पना*

ابن مریم ہوا کرے کوئی
میرے دُکھ کی دوا کرے کوئی

ibné-mariyam huā karé koī
méré dukh kī davā karé koī

How does it matter
If he be
Mary's son?
For all I want
Is relief
From my grief.

इब्ने-मरियम[1] हुआ करे कोई
मेरे दुख की दवा करे कोई

---

*1.* मरियम के बेटे ईसा मसीह

میری قسمت میں غم گر اتنا تھا
دل بھی یارب کئی دیے ہوتے

mérī qismat méiñ gḥam gar itnā thā
dil bhī yā Rab kaī diyé hoté

If I was destined
To bear so much grief
Then O God
Why didn't you give
So many hearts
To bear that grief?

*मेरी क़िस्मत में ग़म गर इतना था*
*दिल भी या रब कई दिए होते*

کرے ہے قتل، لگاوٹ میں تیرا رو دینا
تری طرح کوئی تیغِ نگہ کو آب تو دے

karé hai qatl, lagāvaṭ méiñ térā ro dénā
térī tarah koī téghé-nigāh ko āb tō dé

Pray, do not weep
For your love for me
For it will kill.
For what can sharpen
The sword
More
Than the tears
Flowing from your eyes?

करे है क़त्ल, लगावट में तेरा रो देना
तेरी तरह कोई तेग़े-निगाह[1] को आब[2] तो दे

1. नज़र की तलवार 2. धार

پلادے اوک سے ساقی، جو ہم سے نفرت ہے
پیالہ گر نہیں دیتا، نہ دے، شراب تو دے

pilā dé oak sé sāqī, jo hamsé nafrat hai
pyālā gar nahīñ détā, na dé, sharāb tō dé

If you hate me
O Saqi
Withhold the cup
But not the wine
And let it flow
Into my hands
That are cupped.

*पिला दे ओक से साक़ी, जो हमसे नफ़रत है*
*प्याला गर नहीं देता, न दे, शराब तो दे*

پھونکا ہے کس نے گوشِ محبّت میں اے خدا
افسونِ انتظار تمنّا کہیں جسے

phūñkā hai kisné goshé-muhabbat méiñ ai ḳhudā
afṣūné-intéẓār tamannā kahéñ jisé

O God
Who has whispered
In her ears
The words
That keep
Her waiting
And longing
For her love?
Though it be
He may not come
At all.

फूंका है किसने गोशे-मुहब्बत[1] में ऐ ख़ुदा
अफ़सूने-इन्तज़ार[2] तमन्ना कहें जिसे

---

*1.* प्रेम के कान *2.* प्रतीक्षा का जादू

یارب! زمانہ مجھ کو مٹاتا ہے کس لیے
لوحِ جہاں پہ حرفِ مکرّر نہیں ہوں میں

yā Rab! ẓamānā mujhko miṭātā hai kis liyé
lauhe-jahāñ pé harfé-muḳarrar nahīñ hūñ maiñ

I am not
That extra word
Which one would erase
And write anew.
Then why is it
That time and again
This world does try
To wipe me out
And forget my name.

*या रब! ज़माना मुझको मिटाता है किसलिए?*
*लौहे-जहां[1] पे हर्फ़े-मुक़र्रर[2] नहीं हूं मैं*

---

*1. संसार रूपी तख्ती 2. फिर से लिखा गया अक्षर*

چلتا ہوں تھوڑی دور ہر اک تیز رو کے ساتھ
پہچانتا نہیں ہوں ابھی راہبر کو میں

chaltā hūñ thoṛī dūr har ik téz rau ké sāth
pahchānatā nahīñ hūñ abhī rāhbar ko maiñ

I know not of a guide who's true
And yet I travel
Quick and far
With every traveller
I meet on the way.

चलता हूं थोड़ी दूर हर इक तेज़ रौ[1] के साथ
पहचानता नहीं हूं अभी राहबर[2] को मैं

---

*1. तेज चलने वाला 2. मार्गदर्शक*

دائم پڑا ہوا ترے در پر نہیں ہوں میں
خاک ایسی زندگی پہ کہ پتھر نہیں ہوں میں

dāim paṛā huā téré dar par nahīñ hūñ maiñ
ḳhāk aisī ẓindagī pé ki patthar nahīñ hūñ maiñ

Am I to lie
Forever at your door?
Oh this life be cursed
For after all
I am just not another
Piece of stone.

*दाइम[1] पड़ा हुआ तेरे दर पर नहीं हूं मैं*
*ख़ाक ऐसी ज़िन्दगी पे कि पत्थर नहीं हूं मैं*

---

*1. हमेशा के लिए*

کیوں گردشِ مدام سے گھبرا نہ جائے دل
انسان ہوں، پیالہ و ساغر نہیں ہوں میں

kyūñ gardishé-mudām sé ghabara na jāé dil
insān hūñ, pyālā-o-sāgḥar nahīñ hūñ maiñ

I am after all
A human being
Prone to misery
In the midst of
Adversity.
I am not after all
That glass of wine
Which is passed around
And yet is indifferent
To all that happens
All around.

*क्यूं गर्दिशे-मुदाम[1] से घबरा न जाए दिल*
*इन्सान हूं, प्याला-ओ-साग़र[2] नहीं हूं मैं*

---

*1. एकरसता 2. प्याला और जाम*

نالہ جز حسنِ طلب، اے ستم ایجاد نہیں
ہے تقاضائے جفا، شکوۂ بیداد نہیں

nalā juẓ husné-talab, ai sitam-ījād nahīñ
hai taqāzā-é-jaf̣ā, shikvaé-bédād nahīñ

I cry and moan
When tortured by you
But that is no complaint
Before one
Who has perfected the art
Of torture and pain.
It's only an expression
Of my desire
To be subjected further
To torture and pain.

*नाला जुज़[1] हुस्ने-तलब[2], ऐ सितम-ईजाद[3] नहीं*
*है तक़ाज़ा-ए-जफ़ा[4], शिकवए-बेदाद[5] नहीं*

---

*1. रोने के सिवाय 2. मांगने का ढंग 3. निर्दय प्रेमी 4. निर्दयता की चाह*
*5. अत्याचार का गिला*

اہلِ بینش کو ہے طوفانِ حوادث، مکتب
لطمۂ موج، کم از سیلیِ استاد نہیں

ahlé-bīnash ko hai, tūf̣āné-havādis, maktab
latmā-é-mauj, kam aẓ séli-é-ustād nahiñ

A flood of troubles
A flood of woes
Are to the wise
Like lessons of life.
Like a slap on the face
By a master to the child
Is only to make him
A person that's wise.

अहले-बीनश[1] को है, तूफ़ाने-हवादिस[2], मकतब[3]
लत्मा-ए-मौज[4], कम अज़[5] सेलि-ए-उस्ताद[6] नहीं

---

1. बुद्धिमान 2. घटनाओं का तूफ़ान 3. अनुभवों की पाठशाला
4. लहरों के थपेड़े 5. से कम 6. गुरु का थप्पड़

مگر غبار ہوئے پر، ہوا اُڑا لے جائے
وگرنہ تاب و تواں، بال و پر میں خاک نہیں

magar gḥubār hué par, havā uṛā lé jāé
vagarnā tābo-tavāñ, bālo-par méiñ ḳhāk nahīñ

This body
May it turn to dust
And the wild wind
Carry it far and wide.
Otherwise
Where is the strength
In these featherless wings
To make me fly?

*मगर ग़ुबार[1] हुए पर, हवा उड़ा ले जाए*
*वगर्ना ताबो-तवां[2], बालो-पर[3] में ख़ाक नहीं*

---

*1. धूल 2. सहनशक्ति 3. डैने और पंख*

نظر لگے نہ کہیں، اُس کے دست و بازو کو
یہ لوگ کیوں مرے زخمِ جگر کو دیکھتے ہیں

nazar lagé na kahīñ, uské dasto-bāzū ko
yé log kyūñ méré zakhmé-jigar ko dékhté haīñ

Her hand and arm
Be protected from harm
Of all evil eyes.
But why should you look
At the wounds of my heart
Deep
Oh so deep?

*नज़र लगे न कहीं, उसके दस्तो-बाज़ू[1] को*
*ये लोग क्यूं मेरे ज़ख़्मे-जिगर को देखते हैं*

---

*1.* हाथ और बांह

ہے آدمی بجائے خود اک محشرِ خیال
ہم انجمن سمجھتے ہیں، خلوت ہی کیوں نہ ہو

hai ādmī bajāé k̤hud ik mahsharé-k̤hyāl
ham anjuman samajhté haiñ, k̤hilvat hī kyūñ na ho

This creature
We know as man
Is one big chaos
Of desires and thoughts.
Even when lonely
He's never alone
For in his breast
Lies hidden
A tumultuous crowd.

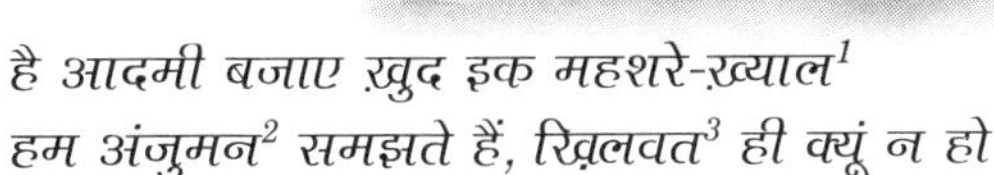

है आदमी बजाए ख़ुद इक महशरे-ख़्याल[1]
हम अंजुमन[2] समझते हैं, ख़िलवत[3] ही क्यूं न हो

1. प्रलय की कल्पना 2. महफ़िल 3. एकांत

قفس میں مجھ سے رودادِ چمن کہتے نہ ڈر ہمدم
گری ہے جس پہ کل بجلی وہ میرا آشیاں کیوں ہو

qafas méiñ mujhsé rudādé-chaman kahté na ḍar hamdam
girī hai jis pé kal bijlī vo mérā āshiyāñ kyūñ ho

Yes, I am in the cage.
But pray
Do not delay
And tell me
The condition
Of the garden.
The nest
Which was struck
Last night
Does it have to be
Necessarily mine?

*क़फ़स[1] में मुझसे रूदादे-चमन कहते न डर हमदम[2]*
*गिरी है जिस पे कल बिजली वो मेरा आशियां[3] क्यूं हो*

---

*1. कैद 2. साथी 3. घोंसला*

ہمارے ذہن میں اس فکر کا ہے نام وصال
کہ گر نہ ہو تو کہاں جائیں، ہو تو کیوں کر ہو

hamāré ẓahn méiñ is f̣ikr kā hai nām visāl
ki gar na ho tō kahāñ jāyéñ, ho tō kyūñ kar ho

This constant worry
About this union of ours.
If it doesn't mature
Where in the world
Do I go?
And if it be granted
Then
How should it be
Why should it be?

*हमारे ज़हन[1] में इस फ़िक्र[2] का है नाम विसाल[3]*
*कि गर न हो तो कहां जाएं, हो तो क्यूं कर हो*

---

*1. बुद्धि 2. विचार 3. मिलन*

شہادت تھی مری قسمت میں جو دی تھی یہ خو مجھ کو
جہاں تلوار کو دیکھا، جھکا دیتا تھا گردن کو

shahādat thī mérī qismat méin, jo dī thī yé ḳhū mujhko
jahāñ talvār ko dekhā, jhukā détā thā gardan ko

My fate
Willed
I a martyr be.
So it became
A habit
For me
To bow and bare
My head
Whenever I saw
A sword
That was raised.

*शहादत[1] थी मेरी क़िस्मत में, जो दी थी ये ख़ू[2] मुझको*
*जहां तलवार को देखा, झुका देता था गर्दन को*

---

*1. शहीद होना 2. आदत*

نہیں کہ مجھ کو قیامت کا اعتقاد نہیں
شبِ فراق سے روزِ جزا زیاد نہیں

nahīñ ki mujhko qayāmat kā aitaqād nahīñ
shabé-ḟirāq sé roẓé-jaẓā ẓiyād nahīñ

Yes I do believe
The judgment day
Will finally come.
But certainly the pain
Of the judgment day
Cannot be
Greater than the one
Of the day
Of her separation.

*नहीं कि मुझको क़यामत[1] का एतक़ाद[2] नहीं*
*शबे-फ़िराक़[3] से रोज़े-जज़ा[4] ज़ियाद नहीं*

---

*1. प्रलय 2. भरोसा 3. विरह की रात 4. प्रलय का दिन*

ہم موحّد ہیں ہمارا کیش ہے ترکِ رسوم
مِلّتیں جب مِٹ گئیں اجزائے ایماں ہو گئیں

ham muvvahid haiñ hamārā késh hai tarké-rusūm
millatéñ jab miṭ gaīñ, ajẓā-é-īmāñ ho gaīñ

He is one
Above all ritual
Above all dogma
Above all custom
And only where
These paths cease
Does true faith begin.

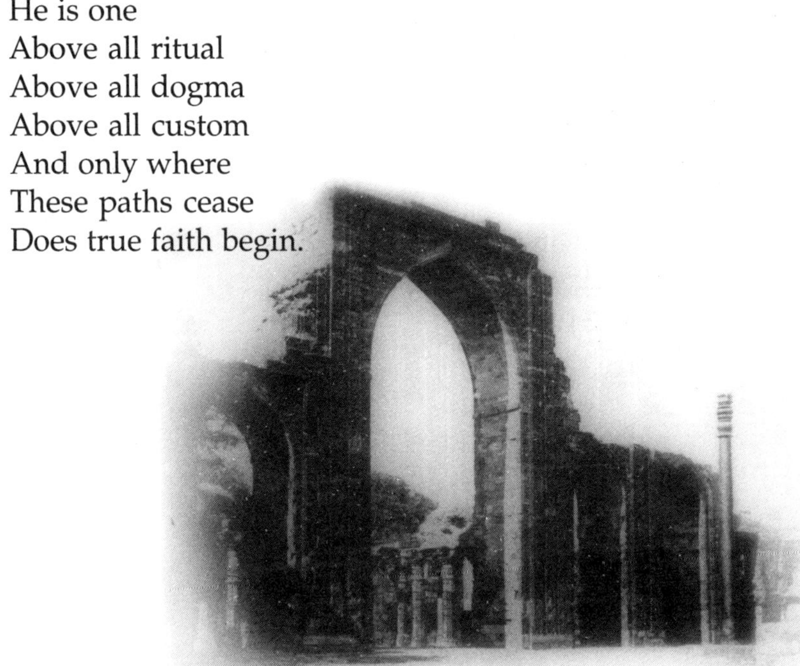

*हम मुव्वहिद[1] हैं हमारा केश[2] है तर्के-रुसूम[3]*
*मिल्लतें[4] जब मिट गईं, अजज़ा-ए-ईमां[5] हो गईं*

---

*1. एक ख़ुदा को मानने वाले 2. धर्म 3. प्रथाओं का त्याग 4. सम्प्रदाय 5. धर्म के अंग*

کبھی نیکی بھی اس کے جی میں گر آجائے ہے مجھ سے
جفائیں کر کے اپنی یاد شرما جائے ہے مجھ سے

kabhī nékī bhī jo uské jī méiñ gar ājāé hai mujhsé
jaf̣āéñ karké apnī yād sharmā jāé hai mujhsé

It's not that
She has not
Kind thoughts
For me.
But alas
When the past
Intrudes
And she recalls
She shies away
From me.

*कभी नेकी भी जो उसके जी में गर आ जाए है मुझसे*
*जफ़ाएं[1] करके अपनी याद शरमा जाए है मुझसे*

---

*1. अत्याचार*

بازیچۂ اطفال ہے دنیا مرے آگے
ہوتا ہے شب و روز تماشا مرے آگے

bāẓīcha-é-atf̣āl hai duniyā méré āgé
hotā hai shābo-roẓ tamāshā méré āgé

The world is a child's play
It unfolds its drama
Night and day.
From where I stand
I see it all
It goes on
On and on.

बाज़ीच-ए-अत्फ़ाल[1] है दुनिया मेरे आगे
होता है शबो-रोज़[2] तमाशा मेरे आगे

---

1. बच्चों का खेल 2. दिन-रात

جز نام، نہیں صورتِ عالم مجھے منظور
جز وہم نہیں ہستیٔ اشیا مرے آگے

juẓ nām, nahīñ sūraté-ālam mujhé manẓūr
juẓ vaham nahīñ, hasti-é-ashyā méré āgé

A name
Just a name
What else is there
To this wide world
And all existence?
What else but a fantasy
And an illusion?

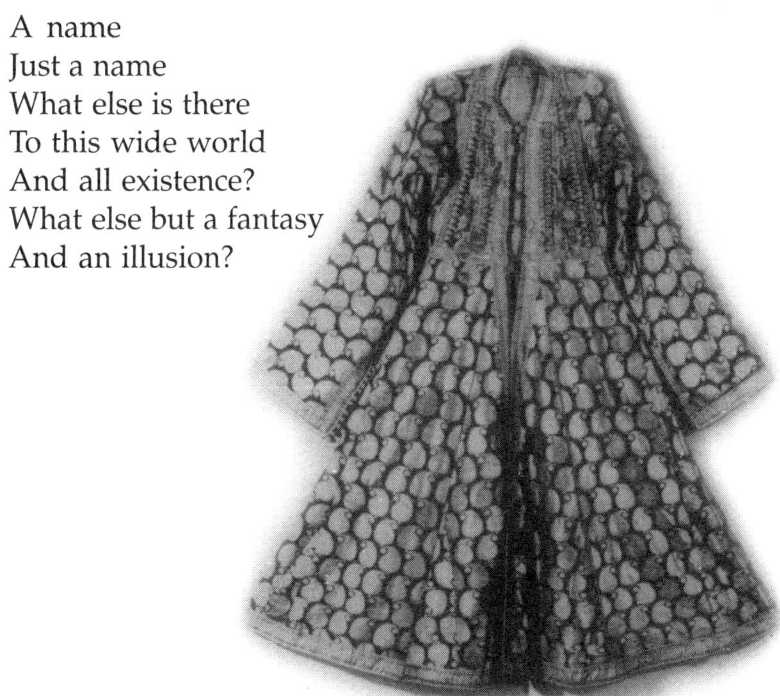

जुज़ नाम[1], नहीं सूरते-आलम[2] मुझे मंज़ूर
जुज़ वहम नहीं, हस्ति-ए-अशया[3] मेरे आगे

---

1. नाम के सिवाय 2. संसार का रूप 3. वस्तुओं का अस्तित्व

ایماں مجھے روکے ہے، جو کھینچے ہے مجھے کفر
کعبہ مرے پیچھے ہے، کلیسا مرے آگے

īmāñ mujhé roké haī, jo khéñché hai mujhé kuf̣r
kābā méré pīchhé hai, kalīsā méré āgé

Virtue pulls me
From behind
But oh
For the pull
Of temptations
In front.
With the Ka'ba
Behind me
It's the heresy
In front.

*ईमां मुझे रोके है, जो खेंचे है मुझे कुफ़्र*[1]
*काबा मेरे पीछे है, कलीसा*[2] *मेरे आगे*

---

*1. अधर्म 2. गिरिजाघर*

عاشق ہوں پہ معشوق فریبی ہے مرا کام
مجنوں کو برا کہتی ہے لیلا مرے آگے

āshiq hūñ, pé māshūq̣ fạrébī hai mérā kām
majnūñ ko burā kahtī hai lailā méré āgé

I am a lover
But in matters of love
Also a deceiver.
And so it is
Even Majnu is abused
By Laila
When in my company.

*आशिक़ हूं, पे माशूक़ फ़रेबी[1] है मेरा काम*
*मजनूं को बुरा कहती है लैला मेरे आगे*

---

*1. धोखा देने वाला*

خوش ہوتے ہیں پر وصل میں یوں مر نہیں جاتے
آئی شبِ ہجراں کی تمنا مرے آگے

ḳhush hoté haīñ, par vasl méīñ yūñ mar nahīñ jāté
āī shabé-hijrāñ kī tamannā méré āgé

Yes, one's joy
Knows no bounds
In the night
The lovers meet.
But however great
The joy sublime
One does not die.
And for me
In that moment sublime
Does the desire arise
For a night
Of sorrow and parting.

*ख़ुश होते हैं, पर वस्ल[1] में यूं मर नहीं जाते*
*आई शबे-हिज्रां[2] की तमन्ना मेरे आगे*

---

*1. मिलन 2. विरह की रात*

گو ہاتھ کو جنبش نہیں، آنکھوں میں تو دم ہے
رہنے دو ابھی ساغر و مینا مرے آگے

go hāth ko jumbish nahīñ, āñkhoñ méīñ tō dam hai
rahné do abhī sag̣har-o-mīnā méré āgé

The hands cannot move
But do not remove
The goblet or the wine
For I can dine
With my eyes
For they are still
Alive.

*गो हाथ को जुंबिश[1] नहीं, आंखों में तो दम है*
*रहने दो अभी साग़र-ओ-मीना[2] मेरे आगे*

---

*1. हरकत 2. जाम और सुराही*

ہزاروں خواہشیں ایسی کہ ہر خواہش پہ دم نکلے
بہت نکلے مرے ارمان، لیکن پھر بھی کم نکلے

hazāroñ ḳhvāhishéñ aisī ki har ḳhvāhish pé dam nikalé
bahut nikalé méré armān, lékin phir bhī kam nikalé

A thousand desires
Each one worth dying for
And many such desires
Are indeed fulfilled.
And yet
The sum of them all
Remains the same.
For no matter how many are fulfilled
The myriad desires still remain.

*हज़ारों ख़्वाहिशें ऐसी कि हर ख़्वाहिश पे दम निकले*
*बहुत निकले मेरे अरमान, लेकिन फिर भी कम निकले*

نکلنا خلد سے آدم کا سنتے آئے ہیں لیکن
بہت بے آبرو ہو کر ترے کوچے سے ہم نکلے

nikalnā ḳhuld sé ādam kā sunté āé haiñ lékin
bahut béābarū hokar téré kūché sé ham nikalé

Much have I heard
Of Adam being expelled
From Paradise.
So have I
Been thrown out
From your street
So dishonourably.

*निकलना ख़ुल्द*[1] *से आदम का सुनते आए हैं लेकिन*
*बहुत बेआबरू होकर तेरे कूचे से हम निकले*

---

*1. स्वर्ग*

بھرم کھل جائے ظالم تیرے قامت کی درازی کا
اگر اس طرۂ پُرپیچ و خم کا پیچ و خم نکلے

bharam khul jāé ẓālim téré qāmat kī darāẓī kā
agar us turra-é-purpécho-ḳham kā pécho-ḳham nikalé

The tall figure
Full of grace
Would not its pride
Fall
Once your tresses
Open and fall?

*भरम खुल जाए ज़ालिम तेरे क़ामत[1] की दराज़ी[2] का*
*अगर उस तुर्र[3]-ए-पुरपेचो-ख़म[4] का पेचो-ख़म निकले*

---

*1. डील-डौल 2. लंबाई 3. बालों की लट 4. अत्यधिक घुँघराले*

ہوئی جن سے توقع خستگی کی داد پانے کی
وہ ہم سے بھی زیادہ خستۂ تیغ ستم نکلے

huī jinsé tavaqqo khastagī kī dād pāné kī
vo ham sé bhī ziādā khasta-é-téghé sitam nikalé

I sought compassion
For my grief and woe
But then I found
That the one
To whom I looked
For solace and comfort
Was afflicted more
By her sword
And was tortured
Even more
Than myself.

*हुई जिनसे तवक़्क़ो[1] ख़स्तगी[2] की दाद[3] पाने की*
*वो हमसे भी ज़्यादा ख़स्त-ए-तेग़े सितम[4] निकले*

---

*1. आशा 2. घायलपन 3. प्रशंसा 4. अत्याचार की तलवार से घायल*

محبّت میں نہیں ہے فرق جینے اور مرنے کا
اسی کو دیکھ کر جیتے ہیں جس کافر پہ دم نکلے

muhabbat méiñ nahīñ hai ḟarq jīné aur marné kā
usī ko dékh kar jīté haiñ, jis kāḟir pé dam nikalé

What indeed
Is the difference between
Life and death
For one in Love?
For you live
Only for a glimpse
Of that beloved one
For whose one glimpse
You do feel
You could have died.

*मुहब्बत में नहीं है फ़र्क़ जीने और मरने का*
*उसी को देखकर जीते हैं, जिस काफ़िर पे दम निकले*

کہاں میخانے کا دروازہ غالبؔ اور کہاں واعظ
پر اتنا جانتے ہیں، کل وہ جاتا تھا کہ ہم نکلے

kahāñ maiḳhāné kā darvāẕā 'Ġhālib' aur kahāñ vāiẓ
par itnā jānté haiñ, kal vo jātā thā ki ham nikalé

Who would have thought
The tavern door
Playing a host
To the priest?
I only know that yesterday
I saw him going in
As I was coming out.

*कहां मैख़ाने का दरवाज़ा 'ग़ालिब' और कहां वाइज़[1]*
*पर इतना जानते हैं, कल वो जाता था कि हम निकले*

---

*1. धर्मगुरु*

تسکیں کو ہم نہ روئیں جو ذوقِ نظر ملے
حورانِ خلد میں تری صورت مگر ملے

taskīñ ko ham na rōéñ, jo ẕauqé-naẕar milé
hūrāné-ḳhuld méiñ térī sūrat magar milé

I would not sigh
I would not weep
And would be content
Had I had
A glimpse of you.
For even in heaven
Among the angels
Is there one
As pretty as you?

तस्कीं[1] को हम न रोएं, जो ज़ौक़े-नज़र[2] मिले
हूराने-ख़ुल्द[3] में तेरी सूरत मगर मिले

---

1. संतोष 2. दृष्टि की रसानुभूति 3. स्वर्ग की अप्सरा

اپنی گلی میں مجھ کو نہ کر دفن بعدِ قتل
میرے پتے سے خلق کو کیوں تیرا گھر ملے

apnī galī méiñ mujhkō na kar dafn bādé-qatl
méré paté sé khalq ko kyūñ térā ghar milé

After having me slain
Do not bury me in your lane
Lest they come looking about
And then are able to find out
Your house and your whereabouts
Only because you gave
The address of my grave.

*अपनी गली में मुझको न कर दफ़्न बादे-क़त्ल*
*मेरे पते से ख़ल्क़[1] को क्यूं तेरा घर मिले*

---

*1. लोगों*

تجھ سے تو کچھ کلام نہیں، لیکن اے ندیم
میرا سلام کہیو، اگر نامہ بر ملے

tujhsé tō kuchh kalām nahīñ, lékin ai nadīm
mérā salām kahiyo, agar nāmābar milé

No - I have no complaint
To you my friend.
But if you ever
Meet the one
Who you say
Has sent you here
Then please convey
My greetings
To that One.

*तुझ से तो कुछ कलाम[1] नहीं, लेकिन ऐ नदीम[2]*
*मेरा सलाम कहियो, अगर नामाबर[3] मिले*

---

*1. बात 2. दोस्त 3. पत्रवाहक*

عشق پر زور نہیں ہے یہ وہ آتش غالبؔ
کہ لگائے نہ لگے، اور بجھائے نہ بنے

ishq par zor nahīñ, hai yé vo ātish 'Ghālib'
ki lagāé na lagé, aur bujhāé na bané

Who indeed
Can control
The pangs of love?
O Ghalib
It's a fire
You cannot kindle
And one which
You cannot extinguish
At will.

*इश्क़ पर ज़ोर नहीं, है ये वो आतिश[1] 'ग़ालिब'*
*कि लगाए न लगे, और बुझाए न बने*

*1. आग*

کانٹوں کی زباں سوکھ گئی پیاس سے یارب
اک آبلہ پا وادیِ پُرخار میں آوے

kāñṭoñ kī ẓubāñ sūkh gaī pyās sé yā Rab
ék ābalā-pā vādi-é-purḳhār méiñ āvé

This boundless desert
Dry as dust
So that even the thorns
Thirst.
And to come to this
Desert
With feet
Full of
Blisters!

*कांटों की ज़ुबां सूख गई प्यास से या रब*
*एक आबला-पा[1] वादि-ए-पुरख़ार[2] में आवे*

---

*1. जिसके पाँव में छाले पड़े हों 2. कांटों से भरी घाटी*

پُر ہوں میں شکوے سے یوں، راگ سے جیسے باجا
اِک ذرا چھیڑیے، پھر دیکھیے، کیا ہوتا ہے

pur hūñ maiñ shikavé sé yūñ, rāg sé jaisé bājā
ik ẓarā chhéṛié, phir dékhié, kyā hotā hai

Like a musical instrument
Full of notes
This heart of mine
Is full of woes
Just pluck a string
And see how
It sings.

*पुर[1] हूं मैं शिकवे से यूं, राग से जैसे बाजा*
*इक ज़रा छेड़िए, फिर देखिए, क्या होता है*

---

*1. भरा हुआ*

رکھیو غالب مجھے اس تلخ نوائی میں معاف
آج کچھ درد مرے دل میں سوا ہوتا ہے

rakhiyo 'Ghālib' mujhé is talkh navāi méiñ muāf
āj kuchh dard méré dil méiñ sivā hotā hai

That ache in the heart
Is more today
Hence forgive me my friends
If I sound so bitter
Today.

*रखियो 'ग़ालिब' मुझे इस तल्ख़ नवाई[1] में मुआफ़*
*आज कुछ दर्द मेरे दिल में सिवा[2] होता है*

---

*1. कड़वे बोल 2. अधिक*

ان کے دیکھے سے جو آجاتی ہے منہ پر رونق
وہ سمجھتے ہیں کہ بیمار کا حال اچھا ہے

unké dékhé sé jo ā jātī hai muñh par raunaq
vo samajhté haiñ ki bīmār kā hāl achhā hai

Even a sight of hers
And my whole face brightens
Oh the irony of it.
For she feels
I am better
And my illness
Is fading away.

उनके देखे से जो आ जाती है मुंह पर रौनक
वो समझते हैं कि बीमार का हाल अच्छा है

جلا ہے جسم جہاں دل بھی جل گیا ہوگا
کریدتے ہو جو اب راکھ جستجو کیا ہے

jalā hai jism jahāñ dil bhī jal gayā hogā
kurédaté ho jo ab rākh justajū kyā hai

Now that he is gone
Dust to dust
With the body burnt
The heart too
Is bound to be burnt.
Then for what do you search
Amidst the ashes,
For both body and heart
Are reduced
Dust to dust.

जला है जिस्म जहां दिल भी जल गया होगा
कुरेदते हो जो अब राख जुस्तजू[1] क्या है

1. खोज

وہ چیز جس کے لیے ہم کو ہو بہشت عزیز
سوائے بادۂ گلفام مشک بو کیا ہے

vo chiẓ jiské liyé hamko ho bahisht aẓīẓ
sivāé bādā-é-gulf̣ām-mushk-bū kyā hai

The fragrance of musk
The colour of the rose
If such is the wine
Who would pine
For heaven at all?

*वो चीज़ जिसके लिए हमको हो बहिश्त[1] अज़ीज़*
*सिवाय बादा-ए-गुलफ़ाम-मुश्क-बू[2] क्या है*

---

*1. स्वर्ग 2. फूलों जैसे रंग एवं कस्तूरी की सुगंध के समान मदिरा*

ہوا ہے شہ کا مصاحب پھرے ہے اتراتا
وگرنہ شہر میں غالب کی آبرو کیا ہے

huā hai shah kā musāhib phiré hai itarātā
vagarnā shéhar méin 'Ġhālib' kī ābarū kyā hai

Ever since
He walks with the king
His gait
Has got
That touch of pride.
Otherwise
What is Ghalib
Who is Ghalib
By himself
And what his standing?

हुआ है शह[1] का मुसाहिब[2] फिरे है इतराता
वगर्ना शहर में 'ग़ालिब' की आबरु क्या है

---

1. बादशाह 2. साथ बैठने वाला

دلِ ناداں! تجھے ہوا کیا ہے
آخر اِس درد کی دوا کیا ہے

dilé-nādāñ! tujhé huā kyā hai
ākhir is dard kī davā kyā hai

What ails you
You silly heart?
What could ease
This disease?
And oh! this pain
What could be
Its medicine?

*दिले-नादां! तुझे हुआ क्या है*
*आख़िर इस दर्द की दवा क्या है*

ہم ہیں مشتاق اور وہ بیزار
یا الٰہی! یہ ماجرا کیا ہے

ham haiñ mushtāq aur vo béẓār
yā ilāhī! yé mājarā kyā hai

I so full of desire
And she so unresponsive
Oh God, what is this
And why is this?

हम हैं मुश्ताक़[1] और वो बेज़ार[2]
या इलाही[3]! ये माजरा क्या है

---

1. चाह रखने वाला 2. संगत न चाहने वाला 3. ऐ ख़ुदा

میں بھی منہ میں زبان رکھتا ہوں
کاش پوچھو کہ مُدّعا کیا ہے

maiñ bhī muñh méiñ ẓubān rakhtā hūñ
kāsh pūchho ki mudaā kyā hai

I too have a tongue
And a voice
Ah only if you asked me
What is it
Oh what is it.

मैं भी मुंह में ज़ुबान रखता हूं
काश पूछो कि मुद्दआ क्या है

جبکہ تجھ بن نہیں کوئی موجود
پھر یہ ہنگامہ اے خدا کیا ہے

jab ki tujh bin nahīñ koī maujūd
phir yé hangāmā ai k̤hudā kyā hai

When besides you
There is no one
Indeed no one
Then O God
Why this crisis
And this tumult
In the world?

*जब कि तुझ बिन नहीं कोई मौजूद*
*फिर ये हंगामा ऐ ख़ुदा क्या है*

یہ پری چہرہ لوگ کیسے ہیں
غمزہ و عشوہ و ادا کیا ہے
شکنِ زلف عنبریں کیوں ہے
نگہِ چشم سرمہ سا کیا ہے

yé parī chéhrā log kaisé haiñ
ghamẓā-o-ishvā-o-adā kyā hai
shikané-ẓulfé-ambarī kyūñ hai
nigahé-chashmé-surmā sā kyā hai

Who are these with fairy-like faces?
What elegance indeed, what graces
Wherefore the fragrant hair,
Flowing in tides
And oh, these dark and playful eyes!

*ये परीचेहरा[1] लोग कैसे हैं*
*ग़म्ज़ा-ओ-इश्वा[2]-ओ-अदा क्या है*
*शिकने-ज़ुल्फ़े-अंबरी[3] क्यूं है*
*निगहे-चश्मे-सुर्मा सा[4] क्या है*

---

*1. परी जैसे चेहरे वाली 2. कटाक्ष एवं हाव-भाव 3. सुगंधित लटों में बल*
*4. काजल वाली आँख*

ہم کو اُن سے وفا کی ہے امّید
جو نہیں جانتے وفا کیا ہے

hamko unsé vafā kī hai ummīd
jo nahīñ jānté vafā kyā hai

Oh that I should expect
Fidelity from one
Who does not know
What fidelity is.

हमको उनसे वफ़ा की है उम्मीद
जो नहीं जानते वफ़ा क्या है

جان تم پر نثار کرتا ہوں
میں نہیں جانتا دعا کیا ہے

jān tūm par nisār kartā hūñ
maīñ nahīñ jāntā duā kyā hai

Here's my life
Only for you.
I do not know
What it is to pray
And to plead
For blessing that's divine
I only know
This life of mine
Is for you.

*जान तुम पर निसार[1] करता हूं*
*मैं नहीं जानता दुआ क्या है*

---

*1.* न्योछावर

نے تیر کماں میں ہے، نہ صیّاد کمیں میں
گوشے میں قفس کے مجھے آرام بہت ہے

na tīr kamāñ méiñ hai, na sayyād kamīñ méiñ
goshé méiñ qaf̣as ké mujhé ārām bāhūt hai

I have retreated
To my cage
And in this corner
I am at peace.
For here there is no arrow
Strung on the bow
Nor someone waiting in ambush
For me.

*न तीर कमां में है, न सय्याद[1] कमीं[2] में*
*गोशे[3] में क़फ़स[4] के मुझे आराम बहुत है*

---

*1. शिकारी 2. घात 3. कोने 4. क़ैद*

ہوگا کوئی ایسا بھی کہ غالب کو نہ جانے
شاعر تو وہ اچھا ہے پہ بدنام بہت ہے

hogā koī aisā bhī ki 'Ghālib' ko na jāné
shāir tō vo achhā hai pé badnām bahut hai

Is there anyone
Who doesn't know Ghalib
But this is what they'll say
When I'm gone away
As a poet he was nice
But a man
Of notoriety.

*होगा कोई ऐसा भी कि 'ग़ालिब' को न जाने*
*शायर तो वो अच्छा है पे बदनाम बहुत है*

پچ آ پڑی ہے وعدۂ دلدار کی مجھے
وہ آئے یا نہ آئے، پہ یاں انتظار ہے

pach ā paṛī hai vādā-é-dildār kī mujhé
vo āyé yā na āyé, pé yāñ intéẓār hai

Whether she comes
Or not
I'm in a spot
For I'll have to wait
Forever
For a promise
She made
To come.

*पच[1] आ पड़ी है वादा-ए-दिलदार की मुझे*
*वो आए या न आए, पे यां इन्तज़ार है*

---

*1. ज़िद*

کوئی دن گر زندگانی اور ہے
اپنے جی میں ہم نے ٹھانی اور ہے

koī din gar ẓindagāni aur hai
apné jī méiñ hamné ṭhānī aur hai

If I were given this life
For some more days
I have decided
I would live it
Some other way.

कोई दिन गर ज़िन्दगानी और है
अपने जी में हमने ठानी और है

آتشِ دوزخ میں یہ گرمی کہاں
سوزِ غم ہائے نہانی اور ہے

ātishé-doẓaḳh méiñ yé garmī kahāñ
soẓé-ġham hāé nihānī aur hai

Even the heat of hell
When compared
Will seem so mild
To the secret pine
Of the aching heart.

*आतिशे-दोज़ख़*[1] *में ये गर्मी कहां*
*सोज़े-ग़म हाए-निहानी*[2] *और है*

---

*1. नरक की आग 2. छुपे ग़मों की तपिश*

دے کے خط منہ دیکھتا ہے نامہ بر
کچھ تو پیغامِ زبانی اور ہے

dé ké ḳhat muñh dékhtā hai nāmābar
kuchh to pāigḥāmé-ẓubānī aur hai

Her messenger
Hands the letter
But waits and eyes
Meaningfully
For certain there is
Else besides
What is there
In the letter
To be conveyed
By word of mouth.

*दे के ख़त मुंह देखता है नामाबर*[1]
*कुछ तो पैग़ामे-ज़ुबानी और है*

---

*1.* पत्रवाहक

ہو چکیں غالبؔ بلائیں سب تمام
ایک مرگِ ناگہانی اور ہے

ho chukīñ 'Ghālib' balāéñ sab tamām
ék margé-nāgahānī aur hai

All disasters
Are set at rest
Except death
Which strikes
Of a sudden
At a time
Most unlikely.

हो चुकीं 'ग़ालिब' बलाएं सब तमाम
एक मर्गे-नागहानी[1] और है

---

1. अचानक मौत

ساقی بہ جلوہ دشمنِ ایمان و آگہی
مطرب بہ نغمہ رہزنِ تمکین و ہوش ہے

sāqī bajalvā dushmané-īmāno-āgahī
mutarib ba-nagḥmā rahẓné-tamkīno-hosh hai

Sing and dance and merry make
But be careful and beware
Standing near
Is the Saqi dear
Enemy of reason
And all faith.

*साक़ी बजल्वा*[1] *दुश्मने-ईमानो-आगही*[2]
*मुतरिब*[3] *ब-नग़्मा*[4] *रहज़ने-तम्कीनो-होश*[5] है

---

*1. साक़ी को देखने से 2. धर्म एवं बुद्धि का शत्रु 3. गायक 4. गीत गाते हुए*
*5. सहनशक्ति एवं होश को लूटने वाला*

داغِ فراقِ صحبتِ شب کی جلی ہوئی
اک شمع رہ گئی ہے، سو وہ بھی خموش ہے

dāgẖé-f̣irāq̣é-sohabaté-shab kī jalī huī
ik shamaā réh gaī hai, so vo bhī ḳhamosh hai

The candle burning bright
Was witness to the night
Of longing and love
Stands flickered out now
Silent and dead
With stains of black.

दाग़े-फ़िराक़े[1]-सोहबते-शब[2] की जली हुई
इक शमआ रह गई है, सो वो भी ख़मोश है

1. वियोग की पीड़ा 2. मिलन की पीड़ा

نہیں کچھ سُبحہ وزنّار کے پھندے میں گیرائی
وفاداری میں شیخ و برہمن کی آزمائش ہے

nahīñ kuchh subhā-o-ẓunnār ké phandé méiñ gīrāī
vaf̣ādāri méiñ shaiḳh-o-barahaman kī āẓmāish hai

Is the noose any different
Whether cast by the thread
That is sacred
Or the rosary
Of the Moulavi?
It is in fact
The faith
Of the Shaikh
And of the Brahmin
Which are
On test.

*नहीं कुछ सुब्हा-ओ-ज़ुन्नार[1] के फन्दे में गीराई[2]*
*वफ़ादारी में शैख़-ओ-बरहमन की आज़माइश है*

---

*1. माला और जनेऊ 2. पकड़*

بیٹھا ہے جو کہ سایۂ دیوارِ یار میں
فرمانروائے کشورِ ہندوستان ہے

baiṭhā hai jo ki sāyā-é-dīvāré-yār méiñ
ṭarmāñravā-é-kishvaré-hindostān hai

The one who sits
In the shade of the wall
Cast by the beloved.
He is indeed
The ruler of the empire
Of the entire
Hindustan.

बैठा है जो कि साया-ए-दीवारे-यार[1] में
फ़रमांरवा-ए-किशवरे-हिन्दोस्तान[2] है

---

1. प्रेमिका की दीवार के साये में 2. भारत का शासक

ہاں، کھائیو مت فریبِ ہستی
ہرچند کہیں کہ ہے، نہیں ہے

hāñ, khāiyo mat f̣arébé-hastī
harchand kahéñ ki hai, nahīñ hai

They may say it is
Even when it's not
So be not deceived
By what is called
Existence.

*हां, खाइयो मत फ़रेबे-हस्ती*[1]
*हरचन्द कहें कि है, नहीं है*

---

*1. जीवन का छल*

کثرت آرائیِ وحدت ہے پرستاریِ وہم
کر دیا کافر ان اصنامِ خیالی نے مجھے

kasrat ārāi-é-vahdat, hai parastāri-é-vaham
kar diyā kāf̣ir in asnām-é-ḳhyālī né mujhé

Some say he's this
And some he's that
So many manifestations
And so many illusions
Of the One
That I have turned
What you may call
One
Who does not believe
At all.

कसरत आराइ-ए-वहदत[1], है परस्तारि-ए-वहम[2]
कर दिया काफ़िर इन अस्नाम-ए-ख़्याली[3] ने मुझे

---

*1. एकत्व की अनेकरुपता 2. भ्रम की आराधना 3. काल्पनिक प्रतिमाएं*

پوچھے ہے کیا وجود و عدم اہلِ شوق کا
آپ اپنی آگ کے خس و خاشاک ہو گئے

pūchhé hai kyā vajūdo-adam ahalé-shauq kā
āp apnī āg ké ḳhas-o-ḳhāshāk ho gayé

Of those who love
Do not ask
What life is theirs
What longing
What yearning
For they are leaves
Dead and dry
Consumed by a fire
That is their own.

पूछे है क्या वजूदो-अदम[1] अहले-शौक़[2] का
आप अपनी आग के ख़स-ओ-ख़ाशाक[3] हो गए

---

1. अस्तित्व और अनस्तित्व 2. आशिक़ 3. घास-फूस, धूल और राख

پنہاں تھا دامِ سخت، قریب آشیان کے
اڑنے نہ پائے تھے، کہ گرفتار ہم ہوئے

pinhāñ thā dāmé-saḳht, qarīb āshiyān ké
uṛné na pāé thé, ki giriftār ham hué

So close was the trap
To the nest
That we were caught
Ere we flew.

*पिन्हां[1] था दामे-सख़्त[2], क़रीब आशियां[3] के*
*उड़ने न पाए थे, कि गिरिफ़्तार हम हुए*

---

*1. छिपा हुआ 2. कठोर जाल 3. घोंसला*

نالے عدم میں چند ہمارے سپرد تھے
جو واں نہ کھنچ سکے، سو وہ یاں آکے دم ہوئے

nālé adam méiñ chand hamāré supurd thé
jo vāñ na khiñch saké, so vo yāñ āké dam hué

Before birth
In the womb
I was assigned
Some sorrowful sighs.
Those I could not take
Have become
Breaths in this life
I am forced to take.

नाले[1] अदम[2] में चन्द हमारे सुपुर्द थे
जो वां न खिंच सके, सो वो यां आके दम[3] हुए

1. चीख़ कर रोना 2. परलोक 3. गहरी सांस

مدّت ہوئی ہے یار کو مہماں کیے ہوئے
جوشِ قدح سے بزم چراغاں کیے ہوئے

muddat huī hai yār ko méhmāñ kiyé hué
jōshé-qadah sé bazm charāghāñ kiyé hué

It's been so long
Oh so long
That I've played host
To my friend and love
When wine flowed free
And the cup met cup
And the whole congregation
Came alive
And was full of light.

मुद्दत हुई है यार को मेहमां किए हुए
जोशे-क़दह[1] से बज़्म चराग़ां[2] किए हुए

---

1. प्यालों के टकराने का शोर 2. दीप-उत्सव

پھر وضعِ احتیاط سے رُکنے لگا ہے دم
برسوں ہوئے ہیں چاک گریباں کیے ہوئے

phir vaza-é-aihatiyāt sé rukné lagā hai dam
barasoñ hué haiñ chāk garībāñ kiyé hué

Oh the restraint
Of being civil.
It is indeed
Years that I've been
Without restraint
And caught hold
Of my clothes
And in abandon
Have them torn.

*फिर वज़अ-ए-एहतियात[1] से रुकने लगा है दम*
*बरसों हुए हैं चाक[2] गरीबां[3] किए हुए*

---

*1. सावधानी का स्वभाव 2. फाड़ना 3. दामन*

دل پھر طوافِ کوئے ملامت کو جائے ہے
پندار کا صنم کدہ ویراں کیے ہوئے

dil phir tavāf̣é-kūé-malāmat ko jāé hai
pindār kā sanamkadā vīrāñ kiyé hué

Let them abuse
For I shall walk
Once more
The streets
That invite
Reproof.
And I shall pull down
In my house
The idols of pride
And vanity.

*दिल फिर तवाफ़े-कूए-मलामत[1] को जाए है*
*पिन्दार[2] का सनमकदा[3] वीरां[4] किए हुए*

---

*1. जिस गली के चक्कर लगाने से बदनामी मिलती हो 2. अहंकार 3. प्रेमिका का घर 4. उजाड़*

پھر شوق کر رہا ہے خریدار کی طلب
عرضِ متاعِ عقل و دل و جاں کیے ہوئے

phir shauq kar rahā hai ḳharīdār kī talab
arẓé-matā-é-aqlo-dilo-jāñ kiyé hué

My heart
My life
My soul
My mind
Oh that I could offer
Once more
For sale
To a customer
Who could offer
Only love
Only love.

*फिर शौक़ कर रहा है ख़रीदार की तलब[1]*
*अर्ज़े-मता-ए-अक़्लो-दिलो-जां[2] किए हुए*

---

*1. इच्छा 2. बुद्धि, हृदय एवं प्राणों का समर्पण*

مانگے ہے پھر کسی کو لبِ بام پر ہوس
زلفِ سیاہ رُخ پہ پریشاں کیے ہوئے

māñgé hai phir kisī ko labé-bām par havas
ẓulf̣é-siyāh ruḳh pé parīshāñ kiyé hué

Once more
That greed
That desire
That need
To see her there
On the balustrade
With tresses dishevelled
All over her face.

मांगे है फिर किसी को लबे-बाम[1] पर हवस
ज़ुल्फ़े-सियाह[2] रुख़[3] पे परीशां किए हुए

---

1. छत 2. बालों की काली लटें 3. चेहरा

اک نوبہارِ ناز کو تاکے ہے پھر نگاہ
چہرہ فروغِ مے سے گلستاں کیے ہوئے

ik naubahāré-nāẓ ko tāké hai phir, nigāh
chéhrā ḟaroġhé-maiy sé gulistāñ kiyé hué

Oh for a glimpse
Of that beauteous face
Flushed with the glow
Of the passion of wine
And that which grows
Into a rose.

इक नौबहारे-नाज़ को ताके है फिर, निगाह
चेहरा फ़रोग़े-मय[1] से गुलिस्तां किए हुए

---

1. मदिरा का नशा

جی ڈھونڈتا ہے پھر وہی فرصت کہ رات دن
بیٹھے رہیں تصوّرِ جاناں کیے ہوئے

jī ḍhūnḍtā hai phir vohī fursat, ké rāt din
baiṭhé rahéñ tasavvuré-jānāñ kiyé hué

Oh for those days
And those nights
Where one had little
On one's mind
Than to think
And to weave
Images of her
My love.

*जी ढूंढ़ता है फिर वो ही फ़ुर्सत, के रात दिन*
*बैठे रहें तसव्वुरे-जानां[1] किए हुए*

---

*1. प्रेमिका की कल्पना*

دوستی کا پردہ، ہے بےگانگی
منھ چھپانا ہم سے چھوڑا چاہیے

dostī kā pardā, hai bégānagī
muñh chhupānā hamsé choṛā chāhiyé

Oh drop that veil
For I do know
It's just a show
Though you be
In love with me.

दोस्ती का पर्दा, है बेगानगी[1]
मुँह छुपाना हमसे छोड़ा चाहिए

1. परायापन

مے سے غرض نشاط ہے کس روسیاہ کو
اک گونہ بےخودی مجھے دن رات چاہیے

maiy sé ghạraẓ nishāt hai kis rū-siyāh ko
ik gūnā béḳhudī mujhé din rāt chāhiyé

Who is the man
I'd like to see
Who empties the cup
For the fun of it.
I for one
Need the potion
To remain
Forgetful
Of myself
Day and night.

*मय[1] से ग़रज़ निशात[2] है किस रू-सियाह[3] को*
*इक गूना बेख़ुदी[4] मुझे दिन रात चाहिए*

---

*1. मदिरा 2. हर्ष 3. पापी 4. खुद को भुलाना*

صحبت میں غیر کی نہ پڑی ہو کہیں یہ خو
دینے لگا ہے بوسہ بغیر التجا کیے

sohbat méiñ g̣hair kī na paṛi ho kahīñ, yé ḳhū
déné lagā hai bosā bag̣hair iltijā kiyé

Now your kisses
Are for offer
Without a plea
Without a request
Now that you keep
Company that's strange
Company that's changed.

*सोहबत में ग़ैर[1] की न पड़ी हो कहीं, ये ख़ू[2]*
*देने लगा है बोसा[3] बग़ैर इल्तिजा[4] किए*

---

*1. पराया 2. आदत 3. चुम्बन 4. बिना मांगे*

نہیں ذریعۂ راحت، جراحتِ پیکاں
وہ زخمِ تیغ ہے، جس کو کہ دِل کُشا کہیے

nahīñ ẓariya-é-rāhat, jarāh-té-paikāñ
vo ẓakḥmé-tegḥ hai, jisko ki dilkushā kahiyé

Inflict on me a wound
Not by an arrow
But with a sword
That it remains
Deep and long
And so brings relief
Much greater than
The wound of an arrow.

*नहीं ज़रीय-ए-राहत[1], जराह-ते-पैकां[2]*
*वो ज़ख़्मे-तेग़[3] है, जिसको कि दिलकुशा[4] कहिए*

---

*1. सुख चैन का साधन 2. तीर का घाव 3. तलवार का घाव*
*4. हृदय को आनंद देने वाला*

ہے وصل، ہجر، عالمِ تمکین و ضبط میں
معشوقِ شوخ و عاشقِ دیوانہ چاہیے

hai vasl, hijr, ālamé-tamkīno-ẓabt méiñ
māshūq-shoḳh-o-āshiq-dīvānā chāhiyé

Better than love
Made without abandon
Is separation
For only that love
Is love
Where the beloved is coquettish
And the lover
So frenzied.

है वस्ल[1], हिज्र[2], आलमे-तम्कीनो-ज़ब्त[3] में
माशूक़-शोख़-ओ-आशिक़-दीवाना[4] चाहिए

1. मिलन 2. विरह 3. सहनशक्ति एवं संयम 4. चंचल प्रेमिका और पागल प्रेमी

دل ہی تو ہے سیاستِ درباں سے ڈر گیا
میں اور جاؤں در سے ترے بن صدا کیے

dil hī tō hai siyāsaté-darbāñ sé ḍar gayā
maiñ aur jāūñ dar sé téré bin sadā kiyé

That I should return
From your door
Without giving a call
But this silly heart
Full of fear
Of the guard
At your door.

*दिल ही तो है सियासते-दरबां[1] से डर गया*
*मैं और जाऊं दर से तेरे बिन सदा[2] किए*

---

*1.* पहरेदार की डांट *2.* आवाज़

غالب ہمیں نہ چھیڑ کہ پھر جوشِ اشک سے
بیٹھے ہیں ہم تہیۂ طوفاں کیے ہوئے

‘Ghālib’ haméñ na chhéṛ ki phir joshé-ashq sé
baiṭhé haiñ ham tahayyā-é-tūfāñ kiyé hué

Those tears
With their power
Will herald
A storm.
So O Ghalib
Please leave me
To myself
All alone
All alone.

*‘ग़ालिब’ हमें न छेड़ कि फिर जोशे-अश्क से*
*बैठे हैं हम तहय्या-ए-तूफ़ां[1] किए हुए*

---

*1. तूफ़ान का निश्चय*

دل آپ کا، کہ دل میں ہے جو کچھ، سو آپ کا
دل لیجیے، مگر مرے ارماں نکال کے

dil āpkā, ki dil méiñ hai jo kuchh, so āpkā
dil lījiyé, magar méré armāñ nikāl kar

This heart of mine
And everything in it
Is yours
To take
But one request
That before you take
Drain it out
Of all my dreams.

*दिल आपका, कि दिल में है जो कुछ, सो आपका*
*दिल लीजिए, मगर मेरे अरमां निकाल कर*

نہیں نگار کو اُلفت ، نہ ہو ، نگار تو ہے
روانیِ روش و مستیِ ادا کہیے

nahīñ nigār kō ulḟat, na ho, nigār tō hai
ravāni-é-ravish-o-masti-é-adā kahiyé

She has no love for me
And yet how can I deny
Her beauty and her grace
And her gait
And all that's about her
Which so intoxicates?

*नहीं निगार[1] को उल्फ़त[2], न हो, निगार तो है*
*रवानि-ए-रविश-ओ-मस्ति-ए-अदा[3] कहिए*

---

*1. प्रेयसी 2. प्रेम 3. मस्तानी अदा*

سفینہ جب کہ کنارے پہ آ لگا غالبؔ
خدا سے کیا ستم و جورِ ناخدا کہیے

safīnā jab ki kināré pé ā lagā 'Ġhālib'
ḳhudā sé kyā sitam-o-joré-nāḳhudā kahiyé

The boat has reached
The shore
Then why O Ghalib
This complaint
About the boatman
Being cruel
And unjust?

*सफ़ीना[1] जब कि किनारे पे आ लगा 'ग़ालिब'*
*ख़ुदा से क्या सितम-ओ-जोरे-नाख़ुदा[2] कहिए*

---

*1. नाव 2. नाव खेने वाले का अन्याय और अत्याचार*

وائے دیوانگیِ شوق کہ ہردم مجھ کو
آپ جانا اُدھر اور آپ ہی حیراں ہونا

vāé-dīvānagī-é-shauq ki hardam mujhko
āp jānā udhar aur āp hī hairāñ honā

Oh, it's madness
But then that urge
Which I cannot overcome
To go there
Time and again
And yet am amazed
At my ownself
Everytime that I am there.

*वाए-दीवानगी-ए-शौक़ कि हरदम मुझको*
*आप जाना उधर और आप ही हैरां होना*

ہے کہاں تمنّا کا دوسرا قدم، یا رب
ہم نے دشتِ اِمکاں کو ایک نقشِ پا پایا

hai kahāñ, tamannā kā dūsrā qadam, yā Rab
hamné dashté-imkāñ ko ék naqshé-pā pāyā

Oh this burning desire
Boundless as it is
What will be
Its next step indeed?

*है कहां, तमन्ना का दूसरा क़दम, या रब*
*हमने दश्ते-इम्कां[1] को एक नक़्शे-पा[2] पाया*

---

*1. संभावनाओं के बियाबान 2. पदचिह्न*

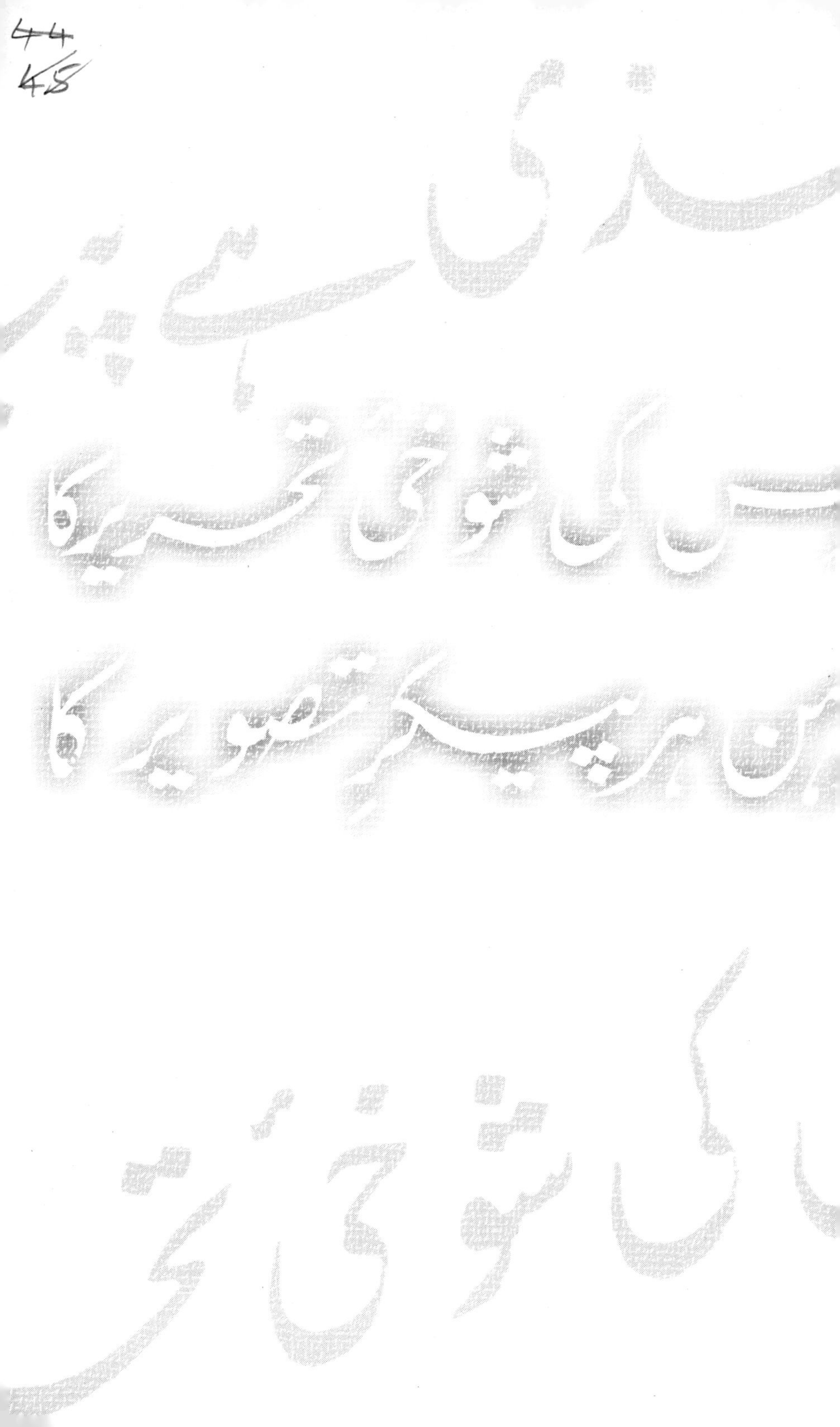
کی شوخی تحریر کا
ہر پیکر تصویر کا